The Spellbinding Power of Palmistry

Johnny Fincham

Green Magic

Published by

Green Magic
Long Barn
Sutton Mallet
TA7 9AR
England
www.greenmagicpublishing.com
email: info@greenmagicpublishing.com

Typeset by Academic + Technical, Bristol
Printed and bound by Antony Rowe Ltd, Chippenham

Cover design: David Walters
Cover production: Kay Hayden
k.design@virgin.net

ISBN 0 9547 2305 8

Reprinted 2006

GREEN MAGIC

Contents

Introduction	How to use this book	v
Chapter 1	To boldly go: The fixed patterns, active and passive, asymmetry, hand size, the palm map, how to take a print	1
Chapter 2	The elements of hand shape: Earth, Water, Fire and Air palms, the shape of things to come	14
Chapter 3	Thick or thin skinned? Silk, paper, grainy and coarse skin	27
Chapter 4	Under the thumb? Thumb flexibility, length and tip	34
Chapter 5	Finding your way around the fingers: Index – the mirror, middle – the wall, ring – the peacock's feather, little finger – the antenna	40
Chapter 6	The biometric blueprint: Palmer and finger prints	57
Chapter 7	On the right lines: The Earth (life) line, the Air (head) line	73
Chapter 8	The Water and Fire lines: Water (heart) line, Fire (fate, Saturn) line	97
Chapter 9	No minor matter – the minor and subsidiary lines: Mirage, affection, passion, mercury, Apollo, mars, loyalty, intensity, allergy, and Samaritan lines; teacher's square, ring of Solomon, bars, other lines	111
Chapter 10	Putting it all together: Intuition, a touch of magic, psychological traits	127
Chapter 11	Different dimensions: emotional, vocational and spiritual analysis	137
Chapter 12	Health in the hands: indications, skin-ridge decay, the nails	146
Appendix	Test answers. Recommended web-sites	155
Bibliography		158
Index		161

Acknowledgements

For illuminating the darkness beyond the known chirological world, I would like to thank the obsessive and inspirational Chris Jones, ex-secretary of the chirological society. Thanks also to members of the palmistry research group: Laura Thornton, Lynn Seal, Swami Swain, Yohann *et al*. Ta very much to my many students over the years who've taught me so much. This book is dedicated to the memory of my mother and father, and to the mad Fincham family, also to Sally-Anne and to Bethany (baby-face) Lea.

Introduction

The hand is the most true, most honest and the most profound window imaginable onto the human soul. The roots of hand reading are as old as civilisation itself, going back to the time of the ancient Phoenicians, some 4000 years ago.

As an esoteric divining art, palmistry transcends its own time, simultaneously reaching back to a more symbolic, mystical tradition, while looking forward to a new vision of human consciousness.

In the late Middle Ages, palmistry was a highly respected discipline, studied at university. With the advent of rational science, however, along with astrology and alchemy, it was consigned to the dustbin of history as a remnant of a more ignorant age.

Now at the beginning of the twenty-first century, the great rift between science and mysticism has narrowed considerably. On every front, science confirms rather than discredits 'irrational' phenomena: changes in brain wave activity have been measured during meditation; the human aura can be photographed with a kirlian camera; even atomic particles, the basic units of the universe, seem to arrange themselves according to the expectations of the perceiver.

In hand reading terms, this has meant science has been prepared to re-examine the evidence: over two thousand research papers have been published on aspects of palm diagnostics on, for instance, the implications of relative finger length on sporting performance or fingerprint patterns as indicators of genetically inherited health disorders.

As palmistry has been assimilated into the broadening mainstream of accepted ideas, it has itself had to change in order to accommodate modern consciousness and values.

The notion of a fixed 'destiny', doled out from a fairground booth, is no longer valid. The fatalistic readings of the past were a result of a populace trapped by socio-economic factors. This meant that any change marked on the hands was almost certainly brought about by outside (a.k.a. divine) interference.

Modern, more enlightened readers are keen to move away from the simple, predictive readings of the past, where someone with 'a line crossing the line of life is likely to suffer either death or great peril from Fire' (from the 'Digby Role', a 15th century treatise on palmistry).

Contemporary readers often call themselves 'chirologists' (Latin for hand study) or 'hand consultants' in an attempt to avoid the baggage that palmistry has accumulated. However, to the public at large we will doubtless always be referred to as palmists.

Whatever they call themselves, competent hand readers are in demand today as never before, as old certainties crumble and people stare into the spiritual void asking: 'Who am I?'.

In the modern global village dominated by technology, consumerism and the media, we can so easily lose sight of who we are. We're all exposed to similar pressures, to endless false and fashionable icons that are presented as ideals, templates to base ourselves on.

Illustration 1 Princess Diana

This wasn't so in the past, when the bonds and influence of community were much stronger.

All too often we model ourselves on roles fed to us by the music industry, by stars and celebrities, by lifestyle advertisements, by our peers or our parents.

Our vastly different natures can so easily be submerged in the blizzard of external messages, till the realisation hits that we are empty and unfulfilled, living out someone else's reality.

Ironically, our fates are now in our own hands to an unprecedented degree, for in the modern meritocracy (meaning social mobility is according to individual merit), the individual has more control over the course of their lives than at any time in history.

This is not to deny that there *are* determining karmic, genetic and exterior forces brought to bear upon us but, with willpower and strategy, such pressures can be greatly mitigated or turned to one's advantage.

To a large extent, character creates future events, the decisions you make are based on the sort of person you are, and such decisions will shape the kind of life you make for yourself.

The person harbouring acute insecurity, for instance, may create a future where his/her worst fears are realised by exhibiting such negative traits as jealousy or possessiveness, thereby creating a series of destructive relationships. A reading which uncovers such personality traits will thus reveal the likely outcome of events.

With enough insight into our natures, however, we can change such negative qualities and redeem ourselves from a difficult future. Palmistry can pinpoint such characteristics and hold them up for examination, so that we may gain self-knowledge and have the opportunity for change. We are then offered choice where there was compulsion. Indeed, the hand will indicate subsequent self-improvement as it takes place.

This book is a distillation of a twelve-week palmistry course, complete with exercises at the end of each chapter. This course has transformed complete novices into highly skilled professional hand-readers and will do the same for you.

As you work through the exercises, you can use your own hand as a template; nothing is more fascinating than to trace the lines as they respond to changes you have made in yourself.

Hand reading demands honesty, first and foremost. You must, as a reader, be prepared to face your deepest fears and know your greatest strengths. This will be the most incredible flight of discovery you will ever make.

You will learn to look without preconceptions, to see beneath the veil.

Human beings are complicated. Be prepared to find that your confident, sparkling friend is actually a nervous wreck; that the artist of great technical skill may have abysmal self-confidence; that the rough diamond you've always avoided may have a heart of gold.

Every individual is unique, a separate universe, yet formed from the same universal elements, the same cosmic dust.

It's truly phenomenal what modern hand reading can uncover, particularly in the field of psychology. Patterns that may have trapped a person for years are instantly revealed.

As the violent tides of the past and future, of science and mysticism, meet in the current maelstrom of shifting values, the palmist must see with a fixed, unprejudiced eye. She or he must call down with Promethean Fire the insight to illuminate the darkest regions of the human soul and reconnect people to the glory of their true natures.

This book is the result of twenty years of practice and research, revising all the available material. Much is original and published here for the first time. Rather than learning a simplistic set of palm markings and related personality traits, you'll acquire a set of principles. Once you've assimilated these principles you'll be able to read anyone's hands with great accuracy.

Take your time. You can't expect to acquire the skills needed to work with this infinitely rich tool in a few hours. This book isn't for those who seek to entertain or exert power over others – the 'party trick palmists'. Know thyself first, read your own hand, approach the learning process with humility and respect.

Becoming a palm reader is very much like learning a foreign language. Palmistry has it's own dialect of signs, markings and indicators. It has rules and a vocabulary to be learned. It helps if you can remain open to the quicksilver subtlety of your intuitive perception. Intuition adds colour and dash to a reading, but good judgement and proven insight must guide understanding.

Look at your own hand for a moment.

What appears before you now as an unintelligible landscape of lines, fingerprints, mounds and creases will soon speak, to reveal rivers of consciousness, the paths and plains of your innermost nature.

You will learn how to unveil the various layers and shades that make up the myth of the personality: the palm will become to you a window onto the soul. Such knowledge will change your life and make it immeasurably richer.

A good hand reading is an enlightening, revelatory, even a magical experience.

Behind that magic, however, lies much study and practical craft. The tools of the trade are here to be learnt by anyone. But if you are to be a modern sorcerer, an apprenticeship must first be served, lessons learned, practice gained and knowledge gleaned.

Then you'll scatter your own fairy dust and surprise yourself with the power of your spell.

How to use this book

There are practical exercises to complete at the end of each chapter. It's important to complete these to consolidate the lesson before moving on. Also, try to test out your observations as soon as possible by looking for examples of various qualities 'in the field'. Check out the palms of friends, colleagues and relatives and take their prints. Try to build as big a library of hand prints as you can by the end of the book.

You'll find it useful to keep a hand reading journal, to record your observations and reflections.

This book will take you as far as you want to go. If you want to make quick character sketches, you could just master chapters three, five and six (the skin texture, the fingers and the print patterns). Even if you can only identify three markers, like a whorl fingerprint, silk skin quality or a short index finger, you'll know enough to amaze both your client and yourself. However, if you want to read with the skills of a master, work through all sections.

Each chapter is like a frame of reference which looks deeper and deeper into the nature of a human being. Each frame must be viewed through the one before it, penetrating ever-subtler characteristics to capture the uniqueness of a person.

You can go as deep as you like into the soul of your subject, but it's important to assimilate each level before you move on.

Someone with a very pragmatic Air (head) line, for instance, (Chapter 7) must be viewed within the previous frames of, for example, the 'paper' quality skin texture (Chapter 3), and the self-esteem issues of the index finger (Chapter 5).

Don't put yourself under pressure to give actual readings until you feel ready. Simply look at people's hands and ask questions to test out your observations, or take palm prints and study their hands at home. Always try to find an example for yourself, rather than rely on the book for any indication.

Take your time – a good hand reader's first lesson is to 'make haste slowly'. You need time to distil the mundane realm of practice into perceptive insight.

Begin with your own palm first. Always proceed by looking for *distinctive* features – if a marking or feature is within normal limits, ignore it.

The traditional planetary names ascribed to various features have been minimised, as many of these associations are outdated and require a familiarity with astrology. More descriptive and appropriate terms are used where possible.

It's particularly important to memorise the hand reading metaphors, for instance: the Air (head) line is visualised as a 'light beam' and the little finger as an 'antenna'. This visualisation process is as old as hand reading itself and is a very powerful technique.

This is the beginning of an incredible journey, one that will lead you down the many highways and byways of the human soul – enjoy!

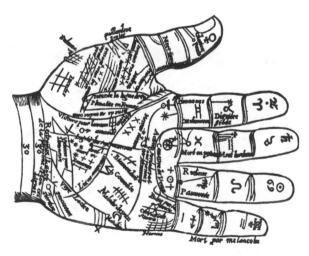

Illustration 2 Classic palm imprint

1

To Boldly Go . . .

As we begin our palm reading journey to the innermost realms of human consciousness, we'll need a map to orientate ourselves. In this chapter we'll explore the territory of the palm itself, so you can navigate the various areas and zones and explore their characteristics. We'll do all the groundwork here, looking at the broader concepts that underline palmistry. You'll be provided with the basic tools with which to begin the exciting business of reading hands.

But, first of all, what's so special about the hands? Why should the palm provide a window onto the soul? Why not read the feet, or the ears?

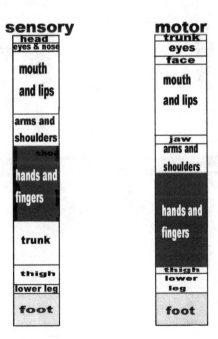

Illustration 3 Diagram of the proportional representation of various organs in the human cortex

In answer to this, one might start with noting that the hand is uniquely rich in sensory and motor representation in the human brain: its relative area is truly colossal in proportion to the hand's size.

If a single strand of DNA can encode your eye colour, skin type and dispensation to high risk activity, there's no reason why the microcosm of the hand can't encode the macrocosm of characteristics, impulses, drives and potentials that make up every individual.

People talk with their hands, they subconsciously reveal through gesture more than words can do, betraying every nuance, every feeling. Hands are the capital letters of body language, they are our first contact with the world. We explore with our hands before we learn to speak. Watch a baby touch everything, feeling its way, trusting the hands over the eyes to perceive the world.

A common myth is that the lines in the hand are merely creases caused by constant movement. In fact manual workers tend to have far fewer lines than people who perform purely cerebral activities. It's the highly-strung, nervy types with restless minds who have a blizzard of palmer lines, proving the point that the lines are a reflection of *cognitive*, not *physical* activity.

Probably the question most asked of you as a hand reader will be: 'do the lines change?' The answer is: they certainly do. The following illustrations will prove this point.

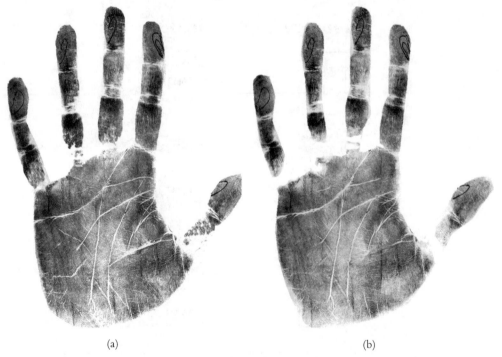

(a)   (b)

Illustration 4 (a) July 98, (b) March 2001

Before we study the changeable patterns of the lines, however, we need to look at the permanent palmer features.

The fixed patterns

In the modern world, we're encouraged to believe that with enough dedication we can become anything, from a trapeze artist to a trigonometry tutor, if we are given the right training. Though this is basically true, the hand shape, dermatoglyphics (fingerprints) and other unchanging patterns, indicate a genetic (from a scientific viewpoint) or karmic (from a spiritual viewpoint) predisposition towards particular skills, qualities and patterns of behaviour.

Ascertaining the fixed patterns is a huge step to revealing our uniqueness. This allows us to point out the personal potentials available and the raw material we have to work with as individuals. Later the lines will indicate how those potentials are actually used.

Active and passive

The right hand is the active hand if you're right-handed and vice versa if you happen to be left-handed.

The difference between the active and passive hands is that the active hand is the developed and expressed part of the personality, and the passive is the formative, hidden aspect. Like the seed and flower of a person, one hand is what is submerged and the other what's on the surface. Both hands change and develop through time.

Its commonly understood that one hand is what you were born with (passive) and the other (active) is what you've done with it. It's certainly true that the passive hand is more representative of the formative years and would be given more emphasis in a child's or youth's reading, but *always read both hands on anyone of any age*.

The passive hand reflects the nature of your familial influences, your nurturing and development, your underlying drives and traits and how your parents and family would see you.

You should compare the active and passive hands constantly. Look to see what is developing and what is fading from consciousness, what's on the surface and what's buried beneath. Try to see a person as a dynamic movement between the two hands and look for conflicts between the two. The insecurity shown on one hand may drive the ambition indicated on the other, for instance.

If, in an adult, the lines of the two hands are more or less identical, you can be assured they haven't developed and changed very much, even though they may have been promoted six times, had three children and learned Latvian! Certain constants would remain in their lives in terms of character, peer group, vocation or surroundings.

Generally speaking, if the active hand's lines are clear and well-formed, where those on the passive hand are poor quality (full of breaks and islands), the person will develop from a difficult start into a much more stable and successful character. This is usually the sign of a great deal of deliberate self-development. Certain under-lying instabilities, however, may emerge in extreme conditions. This may mean that they relinquish their marriage and stable career for a much more uncertain life. When we feel secure within ourselves we may take more risks. As a palmist you'll find human experience full of such ironies.

As a rough guide – the passive hand is more indicative of the present personality if the person is under 21 years of age, and the active is more indicative thereafter.

Always read and constantly compare the two palms for developments and changes, though, as the whole person is the qualities of *both* hands.

Asymmetrical hands

Very rarely one comes across hands that are, in shape and form, mismatched. This doesn't apply if the lines are different, and variations in finger length between the palms are perfectly normal, but where the two palms differ significantly from each other. In several research papers asymmetry has been linked to infertility and severe personality disorders. It seems to occur where the different inherited parental

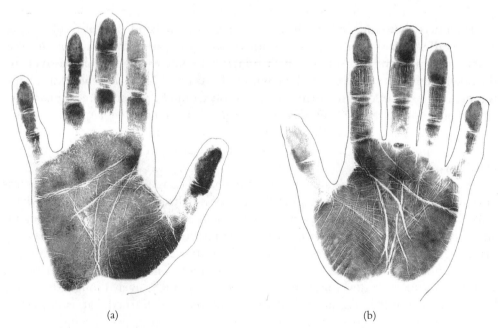

(a)   (b)

Illustration 5 (a) and (b) Non-symmetrical palms

characteristics are 'split' between the two palms. It's important to note that this is extremely uncommon and there should be a notable difference for this issue to be raised.

Large and small

In approximately one person in twenty, the hands are *disproportionately* large or small. Their hands appear oddly oversize or tiny for the person's body size.

As a rough guide, the length of the face and the length of the whole palm (including fingers), should be about the same. So with the base of the palm at the wrist lining up with the bottom of the chin, the fingertips should reach near or beyond the eyebrows. If they are well short of this distance, or if they reach the hairline – and only then – the following will apply.

Disproportionately small hands are found on intense, impatient people. They tend to be a touch manic; they're good in a crisis with fast reactions and no time for details. Relaxation is very much to be encouraged in such people.

Disproportionately large hands are found on those who are somewhat 'deep', eccentric, slow and meticulous. These people are extremely good at details; they can't react quickly and panic if hurried. They're often found on jewellers, picture restorers, dentists and on those whose work requires detail, planning and precision. They like life on a small scale.

Remember: small people have small hands, big people have big hands. The quality we are seeking here is large or small hands *which don't match the person's body size*. This should stand out immediately.

The palm map

Now is a good time to familiarise ourselves with the palmer 'map'. This illustrates the various quadrants and zones of the palm. Traditional palmists used to get very excited about the mounts, but if all the mounts are full, it simply indicates that the person is somewhat fleshy.

It's only where a particular mount or quadrant is *disproportionately* well-developed that the qualities of that area are exaggerated. Even then, we're only looking at basic potentials at this stage. The lines and other markings will show us what use the person is making of these potentials.

The palm itself is split into four uneven quadrants: dissected vertically through the centre of the palm; and horizontally from the mid point between thumb and index finger to mid-way along the outer edge (known as the percussion). Either end of this central line are the two zones ruled by Mars.

Try to memorise the location and meanings of these various areas.

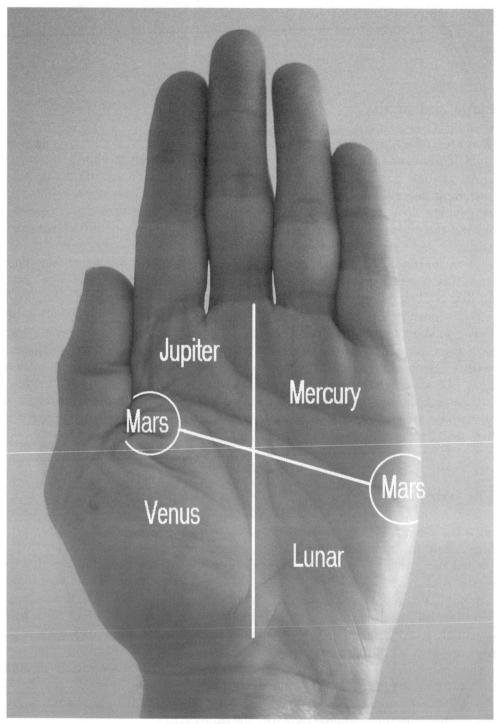

Illustration 6 The map of the palm with zones and quadrants

Jupiter quadrant – the personal world, ego, order, ownership, ambition, possessions, control, influence.

Mercury quadrant – communication, social connections, the outer world, business and financial skills, mental energy.

Lunar quadrant – the collective subconscious, the psyche, the deep 'well' of subterranean emotions and impulses, the 'inner child', intuition.

Venus quadrant – the 'battery' of stored nurturing and physical energy, fecundity, joie de vivre, ebullience, sensual and reproductive drives.

Mars – battling energy, competitiveness, sexual assertiveness, aggression, resilience, defensiveness.

Now we'll look at the mounts individually. Remember, its only when one or more mounts are over-developed in relation to the others that they become important.

If there's a well-developed upper percussion area, under the little finger, it gives the hand a somewhat wedge shape. It enlarges the communicative, Mercury quadrant, giving the potential for business acumen, communication skills and a love of language. The person is likely to possess a great deal of nervous energy.

If there's a pronounced, rounded mid-outer edge, this extends the area of Mars and can lend a battling element to the person's nature. The bearers may be

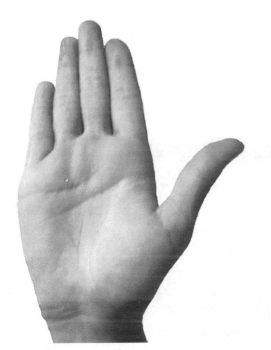 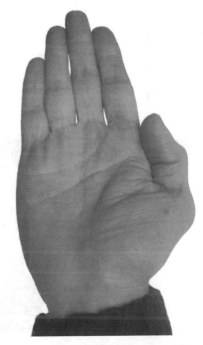

Illustration 7 A large Mercury area   *Illustration 8 A well-developed outer Mars area*

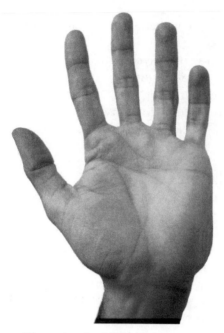

Illustration 9 A large lunar quadrant

headstrong, with a somewhat 'steam-roller' insistence. It's very common on all types of competitive sportsmen. Even on the most passive of hands, this tends to make a more resolute personality.

A pear-shaped palm with a bulge in the lower percussion enlarges the Lunar mount and indicates a potentially creative and intuitive nature. This lends a sense of mystery, a love of travel and the exotic and gentle acceptance. It's often found on people with a natural spiritual dimension, artists, lovers of the sea and nature, 'new age' types and those with a sense of depth and profundity. If both this and the Venus mount are well developed there tends to be a marked physicality.

If the ball of the thumb has a well-developed and firm Venus mount, the bearer is traditionally ascribed artistic qualities. At this purely instinctive level, however, a large mount here gives vigour, human warmth and love of life, with the reserves of energy necessary to develop any innate talents. Almost all performance artists are marked by a large full mound here and, indeed, by an abundance of vitality.

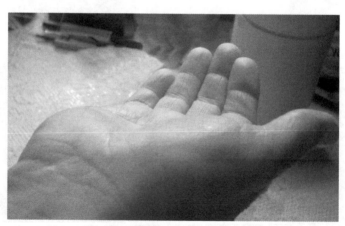

Illustration 10 A well-developed Venus mount

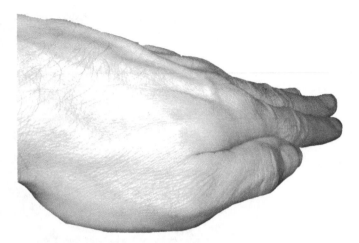

Illustration 11   A well-developed inner Mars area

The Mars mount near the thumb can only be ascertained from the back of the palm. The thumb must be pressed firmly against the side of the hand and if the mound which forms is large and firm there are potential competitive, martial and passionate drives present.

The Jupiter quadrant is never really enlarged. It is only relevant to the meaning of the lines and print patterns on it. This will be dealt with in later chapters.

Print taking

In order to record the changes in hands over time and to capture hidden detail, it's necessary to take a print. Working from a print is an excellent way to learn the process of hand reading, away from the immediate flesh and blood of your client so you don't get nervous.

Use block-printing water-based ink and an ink roller (both can be obtained from arts and crafts shops) and plain A4 photocopying paper.

Squeeze 1 cm of ink onto a sheet of plastic or any smooth non-absorbent surface. Roll the ink (black or a dark colour is best) until the roller is covered. Try to use the minimum amount of ink possible. Roll the ink over the palm, covering the whole surface including the fingers with an even, thin layer. Everyone tends to tense and stretch out their palm while the ink is applied but it's best to get your client to relax their hands as much as possible. Follow the contours of the hand and retouch any bare patches.

Place a couple of magazines under the print paper and press the palm down onto it with firm pressure using both of your own hands. Make sure you push down on both the palm and the fingers. It's easier to establish the hand shape if you always keep the fingers loosely closed.

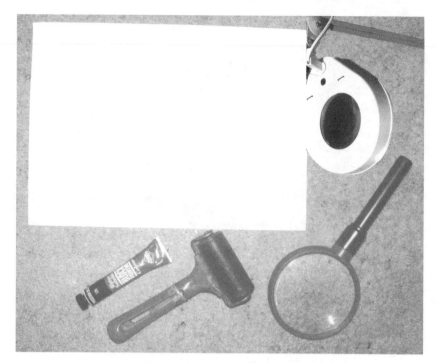

Illustration 12 (a) Equipment

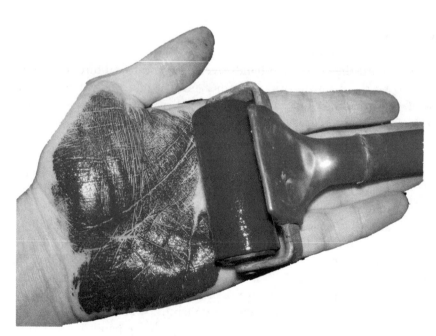

Illustration 12 (b) Inking the palm

Illustration 12 (c) Press firmly with both your hands

Draw around the palm and fingers and lift the hand off carefully, hold the printed paper down with one hand while you do so.

When reading palms, the need for good light can't be over-emphasised. The optimum, fixed source is a beautician's illuminated magnifying lamp. For mobile use, an illuminated magnifying glass is excellent, though it's best to buy a really good quality one from an optometrist. Callipers or dividers are useful for beginners to compare finger lengths.

There's a shorthand you can use to indicate various qualities of the palm that can't be ascertained from a print alone. These characteristics are meaningless to you now, but you'll learn all about them and how to measure them as you work through this book. Draw in the overall form of the dermatoglyphic patterns (the prints on both the fingers and the palm), add an arrow pointing up or down to indicate if a finger is longer or shorter than average. Handedness is illustrated with RHA for right-handed or LHA for a left-handed person. Resistance (stiffness) of the fingers and thumbs is indicated by a number where 5 is completely floppy, 3 is average and 1 is rigidly immobile. Skin texture is indicated by silk, paper, grainy or coarse quality. If knots are well-developed this is noted, as are fingertip shapes (if distinctive). Write out the details of the thumb's length, stiffness and print pattern as the thumb tends to be side-on to the paper and prints poorly. (You could, of

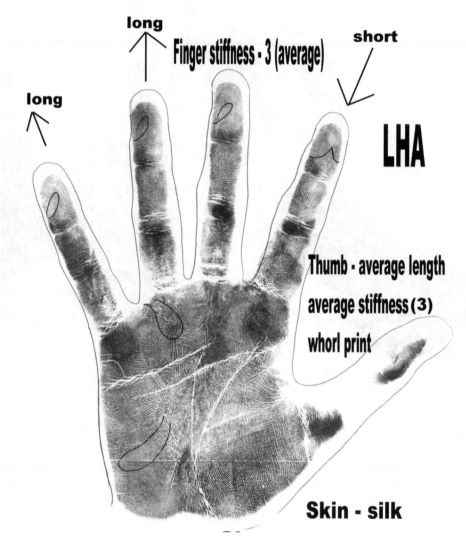

long

Finger stiffness - 3 (average)

short

long

LHA

Thumb - average length

average stiffness (3)

whorl print

Skin - silk

Illustration 13 Print with shorthand to illustrate qualities

course, invent your own shorthand, but these patterns are self-evident and easily remembered.)

You'll soon discover that hand reading is about uncovering layers. It's a process of peeling back the outer shell and looking within, deeper and deeper, to come to know the very soul of a person, with all their conflicts and complexities. You'll soon know them better than they know themselves. You must therefore proceed through the various layers slowly, assimilating the full spectrum of variation in each section before you move on to the next one. Humans are complicated, extremely varied and full of contradictions. Take your time.

It's recommended that you keep a hand reading journal. This is a notebook of all your observations, experiences and thoughts about the process of reading. It will prove invaluable as a collecting pot for all the discoveries you make. Start your journal now. It's a wonderful way to record your initiation into the process. Scribble down all your ideas, even negative ones, 'this doesn't seem to make any sense,' is just as valid as 'eureka! It works!'.

EXERCISE

You're on your way! The language of palmistry is fascinating and great fun and you need to practise it regularly from now on to charge your brain with this new vocabulary. Read through this chapter and all subsequent chapters a few times and transcribe the key ideas into your journal. Take your own handprints and those of five people you know. Look for differences between the active and passive hands and look at the development of the various areas or mounts. Note any interesting observations in your journal.

2

The Elements of Hand Shape

Now we start the process of hand reading proper by examining the overall shape and form of the hand. From this we can infer the overall 'shape' of the latent, archetypal characteristics of a person. Here we acknowledge the concept of the traditional four elements and we have our first experience of the golden rule: if a quality of the palm isn't distinctive, ignore it and move on to the next stage.

The overall hand shape and form is, along with the fingerprint patterns, genetic, karmic and fixed. It represents the primal energy of the person, the body type and the outline of the personality at the crudest, most instinctive level. The hand shape provides the basic canvas we have to work on as readers.

You may find it difficult to discern any particular shape to the palm until you've had more experience. Many readers ignore hand shape altogether as palms frequently lack clear elemental definition and the information gleaned from hand shape alone lacks sophistication.

Whenever in doubt, ignore the overall shape and form and go to the next level – the skin texture (Chapter 3).

The 'pure' elemental hand shapes we shall explore, with their correspondent personality types are, however, worthy of examination because they demonstrate the depth and clarity possible from simple observations.

Pure types are where a set of characteristics in terms of palm shape, finger length and line quality combine to create an elemental archetype. To some extent, we all carry a dominance of one of the four archetypal attributes within us.

The form of the hand is made up of the palm itself, which tends towards being square or rectangular, and the fingers, which may be either long or short.

We, therefore, have the possibility of four basic shapes: square hands with short fingers, square hands with long fingers, rectangular hands with short fingers, or rectangular hands with long fingers.

The broader, thicker and heavier the palm, the more consciousness tends towards the physical, sensual and material; the domain of the body, property and material things, physical skills, and influence, ownership and concern with such tangibles.

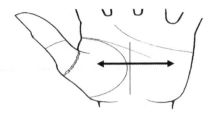

Illustration 14 Broadening palm

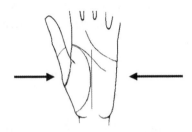

Illustration 15 Narrowing palm

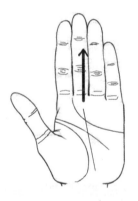

Illustration 16 Lengthening fingers

As the hand narrows and becomes more delicate, there is more adaptability, less physicality and a more mutable personality. When the hand is very narrow, there's a tendency to introversion and responsiveness to externals, one is more acted upon and shaped by the outer environment.

As the fingers become longer in relation to the palm, mental constructs become more sophisticated, abstract and specialised. The personality tends towards introspection, introversion, analysis and non-empirical information.

As the fingers become shorter, mental constructs tend to become quick, less special-ised, holistic and empirical; relative to that which is actual, tangible and realised. Physical and practical skills are more likely to be developed. Short fingers are less concerned with details and tend to grasp the whole rather than the specific. N.B. Traditional palmists linked finger length to intelligence. This is erroneous.

We learned in the previous chapter that for the majority of people hand size and body size are related and in proportion. In addition to this, the longer the phalange bones of the fingers, the longer the limbs; the broader, thicker and fleshier the palm, the greater the mass of the skeleton and the physical solidity.

Each of the four hand shapes (square palm/short fingers; rectangular palm/long fingers; rectangular palm/short fingers; square palm/long fingers) are traditionally ascribed an element: those of Earth, Water, Fire or Air respectively, denoting the basic drive of the person.

Where the hand shape and fingers conform to one of the classic elemental patterns, one can make an accurate assessment of the basic traits.

This is a simple and effective way of defining characteristics, but it's a blunt instrument in hand analysis. Deeper and subtler qualities lie beyond this level, revealing more complex (and often contradictory) qualities of the deeper psyche. Many hands are actually a composite of elements that can be hard to identify, or, despite having a clear elemental shape, they may have diverse skin and lineal quality.

Where, as will often be the case, it's hard to establish the overall elemental shape and form, simply mark that particular hand as undefined. Understand them to be a fairly broad type and move to the next level and start your definition with the skin texture. You will find the dominant elemental shape emerges more clearly with experience.

The elements as holistic descriptions of universal types are utilised to a great deal in the esoteric arts. They are used, for instance, in astrology, graphology and numerology, by Karl Jung in his theory of the unconscious, in medieval alchemy and also in natural and ancient medicine systems. All cultures use elemental metaphors. We all recognise a description of someone as 'wet' or 'down to earth'. We all know someone who's 'fiery' or 'airy fairy'. The classic elemental hands and their respective typology are as follows.

Earth hands

These have square palms, are heavy-boned, solid and fleshy. They have firm mounts, short, stiff fingers and bear but few palmer lines.

The middle finger is no longer than three quarters of the length of the palm.

Where the palm is broad and solid and the fingers short, the instinctive and physical drives are strong. The practical, the material and the sensual are the primary perceptions. These people are truly 'down to earth', taking stability, pragmatism and, in particular, security seriously, often sacrificing opportunity for familiarity.

The thickness and breadth of the palm lends a physical bulk and strength; they're usually physically strong and rugged. Manual skills are extremely likely to be developed: anything from horticulture to hairdressing, such people are natural craftspeople and are sometimes drawn to the less competitive and team-orientated sports. Any skill developed has to be *useful*. The body tends towards stiffness, shortness and stockiness. They value regularity, conformity and reliability, hating to be rushed and often find the modern city, with all its haste, a hostile place.

They tend to be good with animals and natural materials, avoiding artifice and pretension, and have an affinity with the rhythms and vagaries of nature. They are natural country dwellers and are likely to be extremely family orientated.

Inherently, there's an interest in, and often a vocation based around, the outdoors; also in cleaning, checking, maintaining and repairing, or enforcing rules, systems and structures; the home, the body and the garden are often the basis of work. Such hands are common on agricultural workers, builders and cooks. Earth is beneath our feet and often beneath our notice; Earth hands are borne by the essential, uncomplaining, silent army which maintains the system: lollipop ladies, sewage workers, canteen assistants, hospital porters, lorry drivers, cleaners and factory workers; those who are unappreciated and unseen.

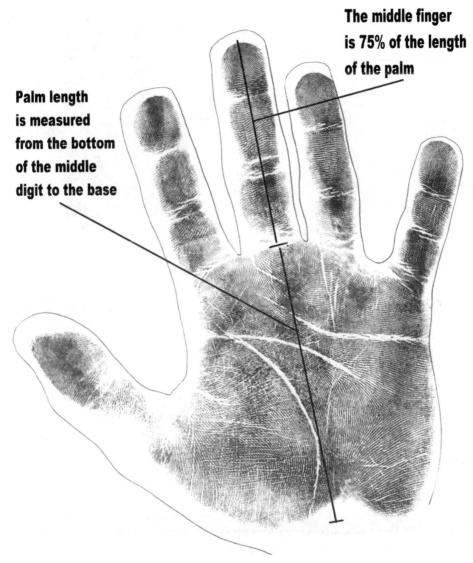

The middle finger is 75% of the length of the palm

Palm length is measured from the bottom of the middle digit to the base

Illustration 17 An Earth hand (note the middle finger to palm ratio)

Change and technology hold no interest for them until they prove to be of practical use, but will soon be adopted if this proves to be so. The tendency is towards what works, rather than innovation, the past rather than the future.

Stubbornness is a marked quality and loyalty highly prized. The instinct is to fit in and support rather than to lead and they make excellent long-term, reliable employees.

We all begin life with Earth hands.

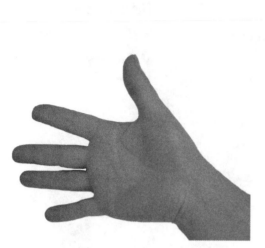

Illustration 18 An Earth hand

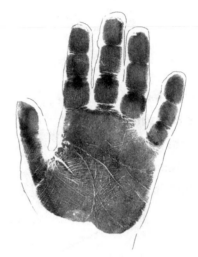

Illustration 19 A four-year-old child's hand

All babies from all cultures have Earth hands. By the age of seven, the individual elemental shape has emerged. It's as if we're initially indistinguishable, with the same primarily physical needs and qualities and we differentiate only after this first cycle.

Water hands

Water hands have a narrow, rectangular palm with long fingers. The middle fingers are seven-eighths the length of the palm and longer than the width. The fingers are flexible and the lines fine and delicate (and often chained).

There is a gracefulness and delicacy about Water hands. The narrowness of the palm means they're highly receptive to outside influences and the length of the fingers gives a distance from the material world. This hand type produces a preoccupation with the inner processes, sensation and feeling. Relationships dominate consciousness and they have vivid imaginations.

Water types are responsive to other people and to their surroundings, being strongly affected by externals.

As they're motivated primarily by feelings, they're not the most rational of people and often not industrious unless the work engages the emotions in some way, i.e. caring, support and counselling, working with children, charity work, the arts.

They can be self-indulgent, avoiding conflict and competition, seeking pleasure instead of pain, naturally avoiding pressure, harsh regimens and strict discipline. Goals are achieved by team work, through connections and by cooperation if at all possible. They can be very self-sacrificial though if a cause is something they *feel* particularly strongly about. Water is the element which cleanses, soothes and

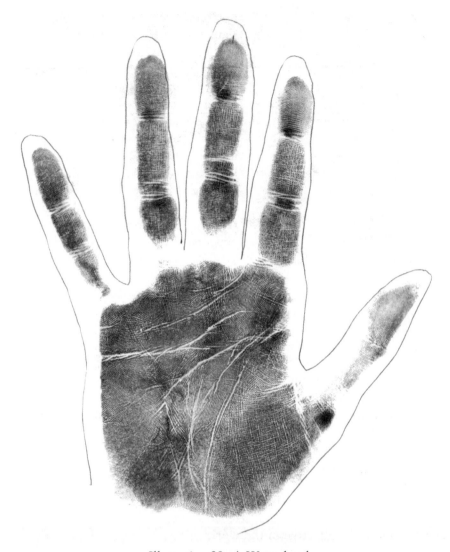

Illustration 20   A Water hand

baptises. Water-handed people are the most drawn to religious and devotional paths.

Physically, they'll usually have pale skin and tend towards the plump or willowy with flexible joints, invariably appearing younger than their chronological age. Whether male or female, Water-handed people usually have long hair. Health-wise, they don't posses the most robust of constitutions.

Water people are subtle and emotionally acute, they're good at empathy and make natural counsellors, therapists and healers. Instinctively they break down barriers between people.

Conflict, competition and aggression are anathema to the Water type, whose sole purpose is to avoid disharmony and to bring peace and equanimity to their surroundings. They're very drawn to humanitarian causes.

Like water they can lack direction and meander in their course through life (also in their affections). They have a need to be with *living* things – animals, children, plants and people. Inherently there's a love of the arts, the spiritual and mystical; anything that arouses the *depth* of human experience.

Illustration 21 A Water hand

Fire hands

These have firm, rectangular palms and the fingers are three quarters of the length of the palm (the palm being slightly broader than that of the Water hand). The palmer lines are deep and red, like cuts.

Here the rectangular palm gives responsiveness to exterior stimuli, but with more resilience than the narrow Water palm. The fingers are mid-length, neither particularly abstract nor too physically orientated, giving a proclivity to *action*. The Fire type is thus a sort of broad 'middling' type, who's mobile and dynamic. They tend to be goal orientated, becoming frustrated if results do not come quickly; impatience is a key failing.

Fire is about the heat of enthusiasm and the spark of the present moment; Fire people seek to change and develop and to be effective in the world.

Fire is extinguished by Water: emotions are naturally controlled or repressed, and any emotional difficulty tends to be dealt with by taking some sort of action (not necessarily the best solution, but the realm in which they feel most comfortable).

Work is extremely important to a Fire person; they often define themselves by what they *do*. Inherently, they tend towards skilled work, eager to acquire the skills necessary to effect change and be fulfilled. They are perhaps best suited to work which gives them the chance to use their own initiative: management, cutting-edge business, sport, motivating others.

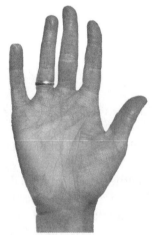

Illustration 22 A Fire hand

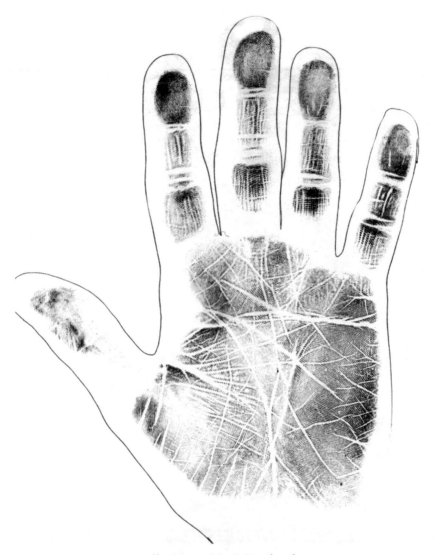

Illustration 23 A Fire hand

They can find small talk difficult; unless an activity is useful, it can seem a waste of time. They usually find it very hard to relax; the best recreation for them is in activity that is challenging and preferably stylish, such as skiing.

Fire people love elites, where there's a special language, a jargon, that is understood only by insiders. The intensity that Fire types bring into life gives them little time for people who are passive or philosophical. Risk is an inherent aspect of their lifestyle – they understand that you can't achieve quick success without taking chances. This type of hand is most often seen on entrepreneurs, criminals and in hazardous sport participants. There is often a love of danger itself.

Air hands

Air hands are square palmed, but unlike Earth palms they have flat mounts are light-boned and have long fingers. The middle digit is around seven-eighths the length of the palm or more. The lines are long, fine and usually numerous.

The long fingers of the Air type means they naturally inhabit the world of thought, yet the square palm means there's a sense of the physical and instinctive, hence they love ideas that are relative and systematic, that have form and pattern. They tend towards analysis, quirkiness and contemplation.

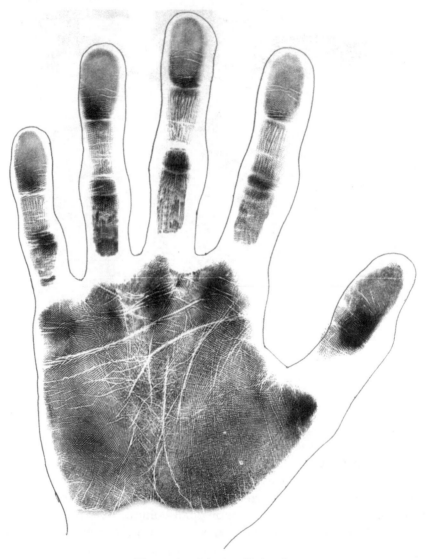

Illustration 24 An Air hand

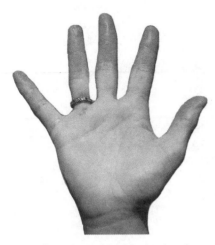

Illustration 25 An Air hand

Thought, study, teaching, communicating and planning are all part of the realm of Air. They tend to be non-conformist and somewhat eccentric, enjoying lots of space. They're natural instructors and advice givers, though often they dislike the restrictions of a conventional establishment. Many Air-handed people work at 'writing the scripts of life', programming the various patterns of human experience, be it through psychotherapy, town planning, writing film scripts and books, programming computers, or as musicians, researchers or media workers.

The physique tends to tallness and thinness. The nervous system is often overworked, as the mind is always active, always thinking. They seek to impose order on the world by *understanding* it. Air-handed people soar bird-like above the common fields of life, avoiding the emotions. For Air people, emotion impedes understanding.

They love to analyse and philosophise. Yet their thoughtful natures can prevent them from living fully and richly. This can give an adherence to principles and theory rather than develop true understanding. Reason and objectivity are the principles on which judgements are made, rightly or wrongly.

The shape of things to come

It's wise to note that the above are pure archetypes and make for rather simplistic readings. No-one is an absolutely pure type, though a dominant facet of each type is in all of us.

These examples are where *all* the palmer qualities of each element are present, so not only does the hand's outline conform to a definite elemental shape, but this if reinforced by the corresponding skin thickness (we'll cover skin in the next chapter) and lineal quality.

This would be a very short book if everyone's hand fitted neatly into one of these four categories so that we could mark out character accordingly. Unfortunately, many of the hands you see will not be easy to define, with somewhat middling levels of fingers and palm, giving an undifferentiated hand.

As a palm reader, at this and every stage of a reading, you're always looking for clear differentiation – areas where the hand you examine has *particular* and *distinctive* qualities (which are manifest on everyone at some level). Reading hands will be much easier if you always bear in mind this basic principle. Any feature which is average, middling or general, such as an undifferentiated hand, is if no great

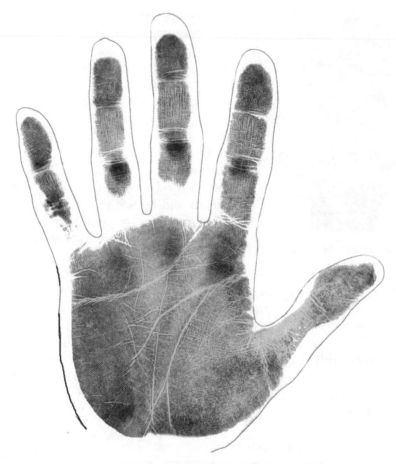

Illustration 26 An undifferentiated hand (one that is neither long or short fingered, square nor rectangular)

consequence. Simply move on to the next level. Even those hands that are classic elemental types will have more complex qualities at a deeper level.

However, the experience of elemental typology illustrates the natural diversity of human nature and the foolishness of our all attempting to attain the same ideals of body shape, lifestyle and values.

Whenever the shape and form of the hand make for a clear and definable elemental type, it will inform at the most instinctive level the rest of the individual's characteristics.

Don't make too many assumptions at this stage of the reading process. In our increasingly desk-bound world, it's quite possible (though admittedly unlikely) that a college lecturer might posses an Earth hand. Despite the cerebral environment, though, at a primal level the person would embody Earth principles: he'd yearn for the simple life; he'd be concerned with the security of his job; he'd be practical and exercise common sense in his attitudes; he'd be concerned about the comfort of his chair and the quality of his meals; his scholastic speciality would relate to the material (i.e. chemistry), the past (i.e. history) or the earth itself (i.e. environmental science).

Similarly, it's possible (though again, rare) for an Air-handed person to be found in a manual job. However, the person would retain subliminal 'Air' qualities: she'd be engaged in a technical or specialised craft; she'd be ruminative and philosophical about life; she'd be non-materialistic; she'd choose the freedom of self-employment.

(a)

(b)

(c)

(d)

Illustration 27 (a) P Diddy, (b) Princess Di, (c) Milosovic, (d) Bill Gates

It's fascinating to see how, outside of the homogenous melting pots of the major cities, countries tend to display a distinct dominant hand shape amongst their native inhabitants. One can subsequently observe how this is reflected in the traditional culture.

Earth hands abound wherever life is simple and where people live close to nature; from Peru to Siberia, all the native village dwellers tend to bear Earth-shaped hands. In hard and unsophisticated environments, only the Earth person has the toughness and practicality to survive.

In the Indian subcontinent, Thailand and much of Asia, the Water hand shape is extremely common. Here spiritual and familial life predominates, temples abound and, of course, the river Ganges is itself worshiped by devout Hindus.

The Fire hand shape is common in Western Europe and the USA, with their competitive, progressive and capitalist cultures which exemplify all the dynamism and expediency of Fire.

Air hands are most often found in the cool, liberal Nordic countries, and in the intellectual and nonconformist circles of any culture.

EXERCISE

What are the elemental classifications of the famous hands pictured on the previous page? (Answers can be found at the end of the book.)

Find a 'classic' example of each elemental type (like the ones in the illustrations) for yourself, and make a print of them. This may well mean you may have to look outside your own world. It's surprising to find what a narrow range of types we naturally engage with. Cast your net widely and don't feel obliged to give a reading yet.

You'll find your Earth hand on a market stall or a building site; your Fire hand where the action is – try the local sports centre. A writer's group or university philosophy course will yield your Air type and a psychic development course or poetry workshop will produce a Water hand.

As a palmist you must have the broadest possible experience of human types. These are the four points of your compass of perception. Every hand will then be much easier to classify. If you're to be a master navigator of human consciousness you must learn to find North and South before you plunge onward!

An experience of an archetype of each element will establish your own 'four directions' of human types.

Remember, when assessing shape that hands are flesh and blood; they're not geometrically perfect squares and rectangles.

Try to judge your own shape (don't be surprised if it isn't what you thought it would be!). See if any of your sets of prints have clear elementary characteristics.

3

Thick or Thin Skinned?

Now we get down to the 'touchy-feely' side of giving a reading. Palmistry is about refining the sensory, intuitive and rational perceptions you pick up from another person and making informed judgements about them. Once you've studied this chapter and developed a 'feel' for the skin quality, you'll have a good understanding of how a person responds to their environment. Palm skin quality is all about a person's overall receptivity.

If no clear distinction emerges from the shape, the skin texture is very often the starting point of analysis.

When you touch the skin on the hand, you pick up a host of impressions. Firstly, check the moisture level. Is the skin damp and clammy? Where the palmer skin is moist on a warm day, or in a very warm room, this is natural and of no consequence. However, in normal circumstances damp skin denotes anxiety or heightened sensitivity. It's likely the moist-palmed person is going through an emotional roller coaster or is worked up about something; the emotions are close to the surface.

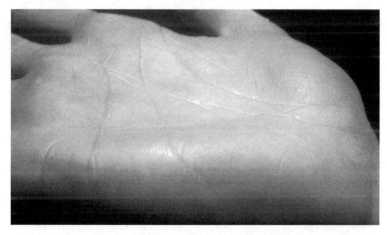

Illustration 28 The skin on the palm is a measure of a person's overall receptivity

Where the skin's texture is rough to the touch *and* moist, with a putty-like consistency, this indicates extreme sensuality.

In general, softness and flabbiness is a sign of lack of muscular development and firmness the opposite; strength and vitality are marked by firm, springy, palms.

The palmer skin texture is very important, as it acts like a filter between the individual and the exterior world. The skin on the palms is extraordinarily dense with nerve endings and its complex cellular structure is actually an elaboration of the central nervous system. The skin establishes what one responds to in one's surroundings. The expressions 'thick-skinned' or 'thin-skinned' are totally valid here. The skin quality tells us what's screened out.

Manual labour will cause the skin to develop calluses and to thicken over much of its surface. However, the natural skin ridge density won't change and over time our skin takes on its natural state according to our habitual environment.

Fine skin is most frequently found on women's hands and the coarser patterns found on men's. The coarser skin also tends to accompany broad palms, with a more physical connection to the world.

Nothing must be taken for granted, however. Contradictions are everywhere apparent. The skin type must be established carefully.

To ascertain the skin quality, you need to feel the skin ridges. These are a series of very fine, grain-like lines all over the surface of the palm. They can only really easily be seen with a magnifying glass. The skin properties must be sensed by touch.

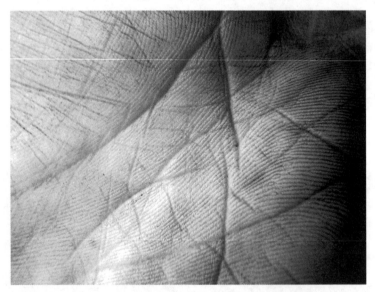

Illustration 29 Close up of the skin ridges

As previously stated, the skin ridges are infused with a vast complex of various nerve endings. The finer the skin, the closer packed and more numerous the ridges present and thus the greater sensory perception and receptivity (to moods, temperature, pain, atmospheres and touch; also physically, to foodstuffs and toxins). The coarser the skin, the less sensory perception present.

You will need to ensure you have experience of all the various shades of skin ridge density to develop clear judgement. Find the skin type by stroking your fingertip softly over the centre of the palm (or an area where there are no calluses present).

Silk skin

If the skin feels fragile, silky smooth and ultra thin, so you can't feel the skin ridges at all, you have the finest skin type – '*silk*' skin.

This is at the most extreme end of the spectrum of sensitivity, and is more common on women's hands than men's.

People with silk skin are highly receptive, sensitive and intuitive. They respond to 'vibes' and atmospheres, tuning in to the subtle inference of their surroundings. They avoid conflict, and prefer gentle, harmonious situations. Usually they're pale-skinned and avoid the sun as much as possible.

It's almost as if there's no barrier between them and whatever they come into contact with, 'no defence' as the poet Anne Sexton put it, 'between myself and the world, nothing but a welter of blood-raw intimacy' (from 'A Self Portrait in Letters').

Silk-skinned people can be fastidious, hating anything tawdry, grubby and base. Men with silk skin are much more prone to sexual insecurities through their acute sensibility.

This type of skin is common on religious devotees, artists, alternative therapists and carers. They're oversensitive to alcohol (though those that have broad, heavy hands and people with emotional problems with silk skin may use alcohol to drown out their receptiveness).

Whenever silk skin is found, it's essential that the person is advised to avoid toxins and harsh environments, and to value their sensitivity.

If you've been able to establish a clear elemental outline from the previous chapter, the skin pattern can be overlaid on the fundamental qualities already found. You can add the receptive qualities of the skin to the elemental character and start building a profile. Silk skin on an Earth-shaped palm is rare, but when found adds sensitivity to the pragmatic, security conscious qualities of this personality.

This type of skin is most often found on narrow, delicate Water hands and the responsiveness is subsequently acute. The person will be a hypersensitive tuning fork that reverberates with his/her surroundings.

Female Fire hands are fairly often seen with silk skin, and thus they retain a certain intensity. They're lively, social people, seeking to express themselves in a dynamic, people-orientated, feeling environment.

Air hands with silk skin are often somewhat urbane, delicate, sophisticated types, communicators of the most refined manner.

Paper skin

Skin that is fine and dry and often slightly yellowish, where you can only just feel the ridges, is '*paper*' skin.

This skin ridge density is very common, found on around 45% of hands in the modern Western city milieu.

This pattern, though sensitive, isn't fine enough for purely intuitive perceptions but responds to visual, verbal and information-based stimuli. They thrive in an environment where there's an exchange of *ideas*.

Communication is important; people with this palmer skin are responsive to sound and images, words and pictures. However powerful the passions, on first meeting they're likely to appear a little difficult to discern and a touch 'cool'.

The paper skin type is so common as to defy specific categorisation, but it's found on those who are surrounded by words, images, paper, phones and computers, as so much of the modern world is – lawyers, teachers, salespeople, office workers, students, writers, and all the media exemplify the paper skin person.

A broad Earth hand with paper skin gives a more cerebral practicality, and is very common on officials, inspectors and bureaucrats.

Water hands with paper skin are common on socially adept and supportive people who are able to express feeling in a 'people and paper' environment, such as a P.A., special needs teacher or counsellor, or as a more academic artist.

A Fire or an undefined hand with paper skin is a fairly universal city type, at home in the modern office environment as long as there is sufficient stimulation and challenge, any lively stream-of-ideas situation or visually exciting environment will suit.

On a long-fingered Air hand, this type of skin is common and indicates the classic erudite, considered type, a lover of ideas, a communicator, someone who loves reading and mental work, such as an academic, a teacher or non-fiction writer.

Grainy skin

The next level in our skin gradient is '*grainy*' skin. This is where the skin ridges are clearly visible and easily felt. The skin is firm and just slightly rough, with well-defined lines; the surface flesh often feels compact.

This skin pattern is rather more common on men's hands than women's and indicates a need for activity and stimulus. This is someone with quick responses, who's easily bored and not prone to navel gazing. They have good reflexes and a sense of timing and thus potentially make good sportspeople.

These characters need to be active and are not really of sufficient sensitivity to enjoy passive–receptive activities, e.g. poetry, for very long. They would find it much easier to relax with a round of golf or an aerobics class.

A broad Earth hand with grainy skin would indicate a grounded, practical, active person – such as an athlete, a skilled mechanic or businessperson.

A Water hand with this skin would be rare, and certainly not 'gushy', but more physically and practically demonstrative in their compassionate drives – like a social worker, people motivator or performance artist.

A Fire hand with such lively skin would demonstrate the dynamic activity strongly – a businessperson, action-adventure leader or army officer.

An Air hand with such skin would be more naturally inclined to communicate mental energy in a demonstrative, lively manner – a media presenter or cameraman.

Coarse skin

'*Coarse*' skin is easy to ascertain. The skin is particularly thick, hard and rough to the touch – almost abrasive. There are very few palmer lines and it's found almost exclusively on men.

Here is someone who responds to the physical world. They have a tactile orientation and need to be in the great outdoors; they're unhappy if confined by the walls of an office. This level of skin induces a rapport with nature, they're likely to be very hardy and almost indifferent to pain and temperature.

The broad furrow-like skin ridges make the person perhaps a touch insensitive and definitely 'thick-skinned', lacking somewhat in the subtlety department! However, they're impervious to hardship, often preferring a more rigorous, un-pampered lifestyle. This is common on farmers, fisherman, builders, manual workers, carpenters, potters, mechanics and window cleaners. They often have a good rapport with nature and distrust words themselves, preferring action to conversation.

Earth hands are the most likely to display this skin type and they often have coarse skin. It makes for an excellent builder, manual worker or craftsman – a strong, physical type.

This skin type is rarely seen on a Water hand, but if discovered would make a good horticulturist or sculptress.

A Fire hand sporting this skin type would perhaps be a mountaineer or adventurer.

An Air hand with coarse skin would be unusual. This combination would make for good physical dexterity, an articulacy of the body and the development of knowledge applied to the physical world, as in, for instance, geology or archaeology.

In old age, the skin becomes finer, thinner and more fragile – effectively more silk-like in quality. Hence we tend to become intolerant of noise, disturbance and toxins as we age.

You may well have only the skin quality to go on so far, but this is sufficient to begin to define the personality. When the shape can also be ascertained elementally, the combinations will be particularly telling. Remember, our analysis is still painting the personality in large brush stokes, still at the level of basic traits and general qualities. The vocational suggestions mentioned are only to illuminate types and fitting environments rather than hard and fast career choices.

On this canvas we will draw in much greater detail later, but I would implore you to familiarise yourself with the fundamentals of skin type and hand shape before you proceed to the next chapters.

With very little practice you'll be able to spot, for example, an Air hand from across a room or on the TV (a great place for hand study incidentally), and to establish skin ridge density from a quick touch.

Hand reading is a practice, not a theory. You need to reinforce what you learn as soon as possible. Try to start now. Just like learning a language, palmistry is very much an idiom of signs and indications which requires regular reinforcement.

People love to have their hands read – but you aren't sufficiently advanced to analyse them quite yet. Proceed at this early stage merely by asking questions to confirm your speculations. Ask: 'Are you a practical person?'; 'What do you pick up on when you enter a room?' If you proceed by *asking,* rather than telling, you will learn much and make your art easier, rather than find yourself under pressure to 'tell the future.'

Many budding hand readers give up because they find themselves too soon under pressure to make blindingly perceptive comments; try to resist this temptation.

Take it slowly. Learn the basics first – it won't take long. Then the somewhat easier layers (lines, fingerprints and so on) are contextualised to that particular individual's fundamental characteristics. You will then be assured of great accuracy in your readings and your clients will recognise you as a person worthy of their trust and confidence.

You have begun the process of narrowing down the personality, homing in on the individual's properties and potentials. As you go deeper, you'll pick up the outstanding conflicts, contradictions and qualities that make up any normal human being.

EXERCISE

Look at the hand print shown in Illustration 30, Print Test 1. Take a deep breath, we're going to do our first reading!

You have already acquired enough knowledge to discern some fundamental points about this person.

What elemental hand shape is this? Adding in the skin quality, could you say a few sentences about this person in terms of their receptivity? What kind of life are they likely to find fulfilling? Would this person make a good manual worker? A good approach is to say what this person is not. Is this an outdoors type? An action-orientated type? What sort of environment would they respond to? What kind of body type is this person likely to have? (Answers can be found at the back of the book.)

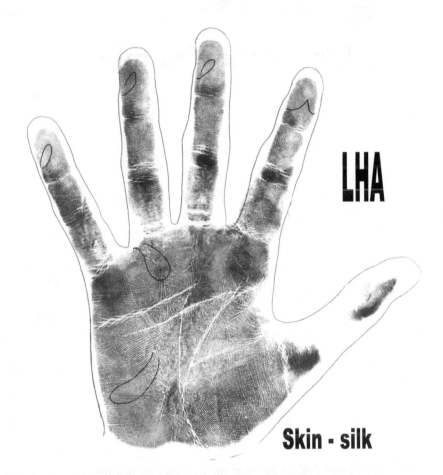

LHA

Skin - silk

Illustration 30 Print test one

Now find an example of the four different skin types, so you learn to assess skin texture quickly. Ask people about what they respond to, ask about their sensitivity and preferred environment to test out your assumptions. Continuously take people's handprints to build up your collection. Put your observations in your journal and write the skin quality on any prints you take.

4

Under the Thumb?

The above expression, like many expressions relating to the palm, is actually very relevant. People with strong thumbs often end up in dominant positions. The thumbs reveal the characteristic approach to life goals.

Like many aspects of the hand, all thumbs probably look the same at first glance. You'll learn here how to subject the thumbs (and in the next chapter, the fingers) to the sort of detailed examination – of stiffness, length and so on – that reveals individual differences. It's the patience and discipline to expose hand features to close scrutiny that makes a good hand reader.

There is compelling evidence that hand and brain development are linked and evolved in parallel. The thumb and fingers correspond to the parts of the cerebrum associated with the self-control, ego, order, creativity and language aspects of consciousness. These are sophisticated, modern developments on the instinctive centres, located in the 'older' parts of the brain, represented by the body of the palm.

The most important digit is the thumb. It's vital to a person's development of self-mastery and, indeed, is a defining human feature (apes have only rudimentary thumbs).

Thumbs provide the opposition to the fingers and our ability to form a gripping motion – this is the key development that allowed man to dominate his environment.

Without the thumb, the hands become passive flippers. 'Had it not been for the unique manner of the thumb's development, humanity as we know it would not have evolved, and that colossal jump from holding and throwing stones to manufacturing interstellar spacecraft could never have been made.' (David Brandon Jones, *Practical Palmistry*)

The measure of the thumb provides the measure of potential self-mastery available. A long, stiff thumb gives the bearer ample will-power to apply themselves to life, where a person with a small, bendy thumb will be more inclined to roll with the tides of exterior forces.

Thumb length is easily measured by laying it alongside the palm. The tip should come to around one-third to half way up the first phalange of the index finger (the three sections of the digits are known as phalanges).

34

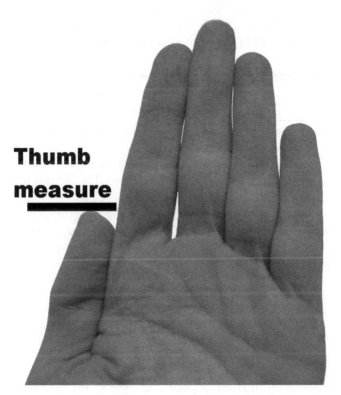

Thumb measure

Illustration 31 Thumb measure

Thumb stiffness is measured by pressing against the lower joint and pulling the thumb gently back.

Thumbs tend not to vary in size too much. Where the thumbs are of middling length, with a reasonably stiff lower joint and a slightly pinched in lower section there are adequate and balanced resources present; this is a well-adjusted average. In reading terms – ignore this feature. In a later chapter we shall return to check the thumb's print pattern.

If the thumb reaches near to the first joint of the index finger, it's a truly long thumb. If it only makes it to the base of this digit, the thumb is short (very rarely, the thumb is actually set low or high on the hand, this will stand out immediately and allowances must be made if this is the case).

A simple metaphor to use is that the characteristics of the thumb give the characteristic sense of a person's purposeful approach to life. A stiff, blunt-ended thumb will have a somewhat sledgehammer approach; they'll be forceful and rigid in the way they apply themselves. A bendy, fine-tipped thumb will be flexible and diplomatic, easing between the cracks of opposition.

A long, stiff thumb will persist though all the various vicissitudes of chance and circumstance. A short, bendy thumb will have less staying power and will 'go with the flow'.

It's interesting that strong thumbed people rarely believe in a fixed fate. Their philosophy tends to be that life is what you make of it. Weaker thumbs invariably believe in fate, luck and destiny.

Strong thumbs are often found on rather bossy people, and not for nothing do we have the expression 'under the thumb'. Powerful thumbs need to be constantly employed in tasks equal to their will and drive. They need challenges, tending to develop a high degree of skill and speciality through sheer application and persistence. A long, stiff thumb is great for long-term goals where rigid discipline is concerned – like training for an Olympic medal. Athletes always have such thumbs.

If you find someone with a particularly small and flexible thumb, they can often feel powerless, that their lives are out of control. Good advice would be for them to do development work in a group of more highly motivated people; thus any challenge or course of self-improvement, be it dieting, stopping smoking or sheep shearing, can yield great results. Such people respond well to peer pressure, positively applied.

Having an extra-long, stiff thumb isn't all good news. Though much can be achieved, such people can drive themselves much too hard, be excessively self-controlled, and somewhat inflexible. Notoriously, they often have little sympathy for more dependent or less motivated people than themselves. They often live spectacularly restrained and regimented lives, rarely slackening the pace until the body yields under relentless pressure. Ex UK Prime Minister Maggie Thatcher has a very long, stiff thumb and is a good example of the type.

Illustration 32 Maggie Thatcher. Note her long, well-developed thumb.

The angle at which the thumb is *naturally* held is important, as it's a guide to how inherently expressive and adventurous the person is. The normal angle is around 45 degrees. If it's held at more like 90 degrees, the person is a roaring extrovert. They'll be outgoing, expressive and enthusiastic and, just possibly, overbearing.

If a thumb is habitually held close to the palm, at an angle of 20 degrees or less, the person will tend to be timid and withdrawn

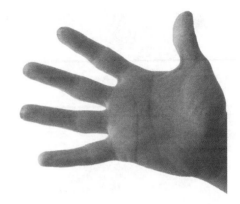

Illustration 33 A naturally wide-angled thumb

and inclined towards introversion. Holding the thumb actually tucked into the palm is a sign of passivity or depression.

The length of the thumb is the amount of potential oppositional strength to the natural impulses the person has. The stiffness of the lower joint is how rigidly they apply themselves. A small, stiff thumb will generally achieve more than a long, bendy one. Stiffness will quickly develop when one applies oneself assiduously to a long-term goal.

Bendy-thumbed people are child-like and easygoing; they like to linger and smell the roses on the journey of life. This more laid-back, open, spontaneous type of thumb is very common on musicians, entertainers, 'people people' and on actors. They need variety and stimulus to sweeten their labours.

Occasionally, one may find a naturally curved-back thumb which is flexible at the first joint, but stiff at the base. This denotes someone whose energy comes in circles. They tend to drop on-going tasks and return to them later, often many months later, but persistence is present, as is the ability to approach a project from various angles.

Where the thumb is extremely floppy and flexible at the base (so that it can be bent back almost to touch the wrist) it's known as hyperflexive. People are often proud of their hyperflexive thumbs

Illustration 34 A thumb which is flexible at the first joint, but stiff at the base

Illustration 35 A hyperflexive thumb

and demonstrate them at every opportunity. However, this amount of flexibility signals an over-adaptable nature, someone lacking staying power and who needs constant change and stimulation.

It's a bonus for an actor, for example, where one has to constantly adapt to new roles and one is driven externally to accommodate the demands of script or director – but they can 'bend over backwards' for others and be far too accommodating. Too much time and energy is spent appeasing others.

Usually, hyperflexive thumbs have a need for great deal of freedom in everything, and hate regimentation. Incidentally, this is also a sign of early onset of joint and ligament problems, particularly in the spine.

Applying oneself to a disciplined course of physical activity will develop greater stiffness at the lower joint, so advise this course of action to all hyperflexive thumbs.

The sections of the digits are known as phalanges. The lower thumb phalange acts like a mustering post for the force applied through the top phalange. The two sections are usually roughly equal in size or the top section is slightly larger. When the bottom phalange is much longer than the top, and particularly if it's also broad, there can be excessive planning and rumination and little action. This is common on planners, private detectives, computer programmers and pedants – people who need to analyse and ponder before execution. This can lead to an argumentative bluntness, a reliance on 'the facts'.

Usually there's a slightly pinched in section to the lower phalange, giving an 'egg-timer' effect. The more this phalange narrows, the more spontaneous the drive and the more one wants to act with little preparation.

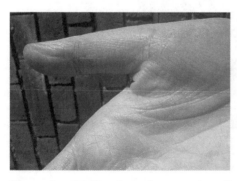

Illustration 36 Dominant lower section of thumb

The tip of the thumb is usually rounded. When it's spatulate (blunt-ended and broad at the tip), there are usually mechanical or practical abilities.

If clubbed, with a bulbous, thick tip, there's a raw passion present. This is very common on drummers, physical people, dancers, wrestlers, midwives and martial artists. It gives a need for a direct, physical dimension to experience and adds a restless intensity to even the most refined hand. There's a touch of the primal in these blunderbuss-like thumbs.

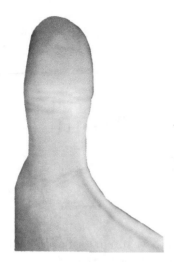

Illustration 37 'Pinched in' lower section of thumb

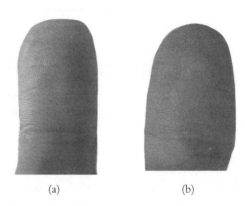

(a)　　　　　　　　(b)

Illustration 38 (a) A spatulate thumb, and (b) an average-tipped thumb

It's fascinating to watch the way in which different thumb types approach, say, giving up smoking. The bendy thumb will abstain in conjunction with a friend, nicotine patches and support group; the long base phalange thumb will study all the literature and prepare for the encounter with meticulous thoroughness; the short thumb will put off the date as long as possible; long, stiff thumbs set a date and simply go 'cold turkey'.

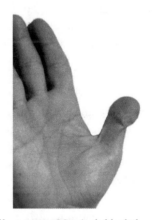

Illustration 39 A clubbed thumb

EXERCISE

According to tradition, Hindu palmists only read the thumbs. Check the length, stiffness and phalange balance of ten people's thumbs. Compare the active and passive – you'll find the active hand thumb very slightly bigger and stiffer. Mark the thumb's qualities (length, stiffness, tip shape, if distinctive) on any prints you take. Try to find some examples of definite thumb characteristics, i.e. extra long, extra short, hyperflexive, very stiff. Note your findings in your journal.

5

Finding Your Way Around the Fingers

However average or individual you may have found a palm in terms of its shape and thumb characteristics, you'll definitely find something distinctive in this chapter, as everyone has some unique quality to their digits. The fingers provide a wonderfully rich reservoir of information in terms of an individual's psychology, motivations, drives and background. You'll find your way around the fingers much easier if you reinforce each finger's qualities by using its metaphor.

Treat each finger as a separate section. Re-read each section as necessary to consolidate your understanding before you go on to the next. Examine your own fingers in the light of the text to help assimilate the information.

The thumb and digits barely change in relation to each other through the life cycle. Subtle changes occur during physical development and as old age progresses the fingers may collapse and bend with the onset of rheumatic conditions and bone shrinkage. To measure the relative length of the fingers, it's important to make sure they're extending vertically from the body of the palm; any leaning will distort their natural balance.

The average and standard relative lengths of the fingers are: The index and ring fingers are of the same length (or with the index shorter by up to half a centimetre). You can check this by standing a straight edge across the top of these digits and bending the middle finger out of the way. If the ruler's level the fingers are the same length. Its angle will tell you how severe the imbalance in length is between them. If you find it hard to measure by eye alone, use callipers or a ruler to measure the height of each.

The middle finger's average length is for half it's top phalange to protrude between the digits either side. The little finger's measure is for it to reach the crease line of the top phalange of the ring finger.

After some practice, an over-long or short digit will stand out immediately, but do use callipers or a ruler initially if you're not sure.

The fingers indicate aspects of distinct mental faculties, each one accounting for a large area of the cerebrum. They reveal a vast amount about our fundamental attitudes, our formative development and the roles we play in life.

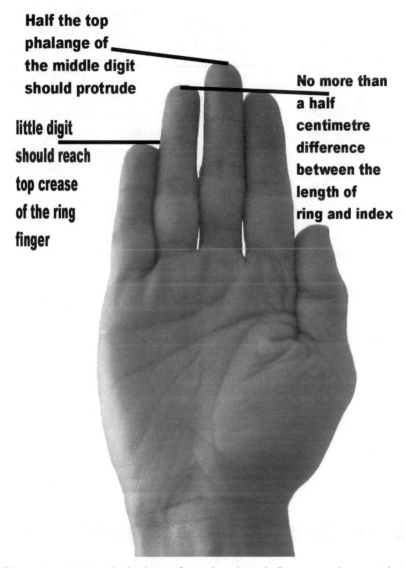

Half the top phalange of the middle digit should protrude

No more than a half centimetre difference between the length of ring and index

little digit should reach top crease of the ring finger

Illustration 40 Standard relative finger length with fingers standing upright from the palm

If the thumb is held naturally wide-angled, the fingers are also likely to be spontaneously well spread. An expressive, extroverted nature is revealed if they're habitually positioned like this. The spread-fingered person tends to be bold and afraid of nothing.

Naturally closed-together fingers, however, are a sign of inhibition and caution Note the natural spread and angle of the digits before you take a print of them.

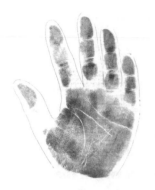

Illustration 41 All digits leaning towards the thumb

Occasionally, all the digits may bear a distinct leaning to the thumb side. Here the person has a serious lack internally. There's no inner life, no balance; they're literally toppling over through dependence on partner, life role, career, family or the need to be needed.

People with this pattern don't like being alone and constantly refer to some 'other,' some external that gives them a sense of self. No-one with this inner vacuum enjoys having this pointed out to them and they will often be highly resistant to facing this point.

It is very common on carers, partners of prestigious people and people whose appearance and lifestyle creates a ready-made personality. This is the mark of a superficial personality who's in constant demand, but one that's liable to collapse when the external framework disappears.

They should be gently encouraged to develop their own ideas and values and take responsibility for themselves, along with the development of an inner life. This leaning indicates the likelihood of 'burn out' type illnesses, such as M.E. or simple physical exhaustion, and often there are postural problems.

Much rarer is where all the fingers lean towards the little finger side. This is a withdrawal from life; the introverted existence of the classic 'anorak'. Here, every impulse is held in, they don't want to deal with real life and much prefer fantasy or some very personal world. This is common on social misfits, withdrawn personal-

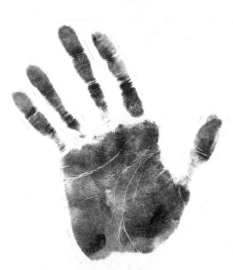

Illustration 42 All fingers leaning away from the thumb

ities and spiritually inclined or escapist people who prefer a closeted existence.

Advice should be given to encourage their emergence to the outer world, preferably through the illumination of some talent or skill found elsewhere on the hand.

The amount of flexibility of the fingers (how much they can bend backward when pressure is applied) must also be taken into account. The fingers tend to be naturally fixed on Earth palms and, of course, will lack movement where arthritis or joint problems are present. Fingers which hardly move more than 10 degrees beyond the vertical in other cases, however, represent a locked-up body generally; high, long-term stress levels; rigid mental processes and a resistance to acting spontaneously. It's a sign of feeling under pressure.

In the opposite case, where the fingers are very floppy and free, extending back 45 degrees or more, the body itself is free and flexible and the person tends to be very spontaneous. They'll be extremely open psychologically and often attempt to do too many things at once. They may well lack structure; freedom comes before everything. Such people are actually much more successful when given structure. Hyperflexive fingered people have a much greater incidence of ligament and joint problems, particularly RSI.

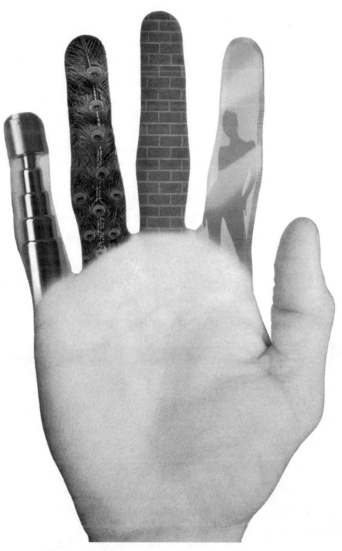

Illustration 43 Metaphorical depiction of digits

The digits in palmistry have traditionally been allocated planetary names and attributes; namely those of Jupiter (index), Saturn (middle), Apollo (ring), and Mercury (little finger).

The fingers represent aspects of the cerebral cortex relating to self-consciousness (index), values (middle), social expression (ring), and communication (little finger).

A far more appropriate way to visualise the digits is to use the metaphors of the **mirror** of self-consciousness (index), the **wall** of value systems (middle), the **peacock's feather** of persona (ring) and the **antenna** of communication (little finger).

Index finger – the mirror

This is the most important digit, as it's the finger of self-reflection. This finger represents the relationship you have with yourself and your self-consciousness. It rules the personal world, self-advancement, self-esteem and personal vision. Responsibility and integrity are also connected with this digit.

Its measure is in comparison with the ring finger.

If the mirror digit is the same length, or up to half a centimetre shorter than the ring finger, and if it's also straight – average, balanced qualities are presented. Move on to another feature.

If it's only so much as a millimetre longer than the ring finger, it's considered long. Long mirror fingers tend to be latent or overt control-freaks. They indulge in much self-reflection and are intensely self-aware. They also possess a natural sense of authority.

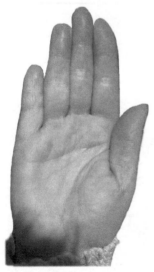

Illustration 44 A long 'mirror' digit

They're willing to work hard to achieve their personal goals, because they have personal vision and see themselves worthy of the high standards they set themselves.

It has been proven that cortex development is shaped to a great extent in early childhood as a response to the emotive reinforcement provided by the carer figure (Greenough, Black and Wallace 1987). Also, ring and index digit development has been linked to residual testosterone and oestrogen levels (Manning J. 'Sex role identity related to ratio of 2nd and 4th digit', *Biological Psychology*, February 2003). Thus, much can be ascertained about early development by the relative length of these digits.

When the mirror digit is long (relative to the ring finger) on the passive hand, the person developed during childhood an overt awareness of themselves and the consequences of their actions. This is much more common on only children, the precocious eldest or youngest in the family, on children with highly expectant parents, or where they had to fill the role of an absent or incompetent mother figure. Invariably their mother was exceptionally strong and well respected or there was no effective mother figure, so they had to develop a responsible role for themselves at a young age.

Long mirror digits tend to take themselves too seriously. They'd much prefer to run their own world the way they want than sacrifice their values for such superficial things as 'fame' or popularity. They naturally mistrust the flashy and ostentatious and are innately conservative (and usually a little self-obsessed).

They are, however, innately sincere souls with high ideals, personal ambitions and standards they really care about. They very often end up with great responsibilities and in influential positions, bearing such burdens with aplomb.

When (as is usual) this feature is accompanied by a strong thumb and clear lines, high attainments are guaranteed, particularly in a personal working environment where autonomy, responsibility, diplomatic, social and organisational skills are required, e.g. a head teacher, running a small personal business, counsellor.

The long 'mirror' gives an exaggerated sense of self and magnifies one's own flaws. Hence there can be much self-criticism, perfectionism and a perennial sense of striving to get the respect and ideals required.

Where there is a weak thumb and poor lines, long index finger types can be highly manipulative as a means of gaining control and influence, particularly over their partners.

The difference between a long ring finger and a long index is the crucial difference between an exaggerated public persona (long peacock's feather) and exaggerated private self awareness and ambition (long mirror); between gaining attention by 'playing up' (peacock's feather) or by gaining influence by developing precocious self-reliance (mirror). A long *peacock's feather* finger is often splendid at 'working a crowd', with boundless apparent public confidence, where a long *mirror* digit is better with smaller groups and in one-to-one situations where their high standards can be applied.

As will be seen when we discuss the ring finger, public confidence is very different to personal self-esteem.

Where the index finger is more than the standard half-centimetre shorter than the ring finger, the person suffers deep-held feelings of inadequacy. The shorter the 'mirror' finger, the more the reflected self-image is diminutive.

In these cases, there's an aversion to self-analysis and a lack of early responsibility and authority. It's common in children of large families where one had to play up to get attention and in any situation where self-value and responsibility wasn't reinforced (usually a sign of parental neglect or of being 'spoilt', or from not being given a sense of individuality). A short index is usually more pronounced on the passive hand and indicates the development of greater self-worth in maturity.

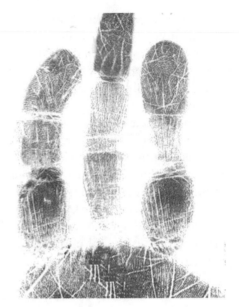

Illustration 45 A very short 'mirror' digit   *Illustration 46 A bent index digit*

Depression and self-neglect, health and weight problems have been linked to this trait (Manning J. 'Depression index' *American Journal of Evolution and Behaviour*, September 2000). One benefit of the finger being weak, however, is that one's private sense of self is more easily hidden behind the public face.

When, as in Illustration 45, this finger is very short and if it's accompanied by a very long ring finger, there's often massive over-compensation going on. This is typical of a 'larger than life' personality; a need to 'shout' to be noticed. From portraits and imprints of the hands of Hitler, Napoleon and most historically infamous figures, it can be observed that this trait is extremely marked.

The limited self-value of these personalities emboldened them to take huge risks, they felt (to themselves) of little consequence. This was the secret of their triumphs and the cause of their eventual defeats.

Always encourage such people to value themselves.

A bend in a digit weakens it and has the effect of making it shorter. If the index is bent towards the middle digit, this shows one's sense of self is relative to job, family or authority and is readily sublimated into some greater structure, often with considerable success.

This is very common on the diligent 'number two' in an organisation and it signals a need to belong and be associated with an exterior structure. The crucial point here is that status or authority is conferred by others, but lack of self-belief and singular confidence is apparent. A bent short index finger and a long ring finger is endemic in showbiz.

Middle finger – the wall

This is, of course, the longest digit and it's the finger of psychological stability, values and balance. If of normal length and straight it can be assessed as adequate and average and consequently ignored.

Its metaphor is the 'wall', as it represents the fixed, 'weighty' and serious mental constructs. Such concepts as patriarchy, orthodoxy, lifestyle, rules, restrictions, authority, career, convention and what values you live by are established here. Such fixed, certain constructs form our mental boundaries and logical ideas which fit like bricks into a system.

On the passive hand, this digit is more representative of the values of the formative environment – family, schooling, material security and tradition.

Its normal length is for half the top phalange to stand proud of the digits either side, so the base of the middle digit's nail is at roughly equal height to a line drawn across the tips of the neighbouring (index and ring) digits.

This finger is very often bent (on around 27% of hands). We live in a time when boundaries, walls and value systems are collapsing and this is the reflected effect. You might see this sign as a wavering from the orthodox in modern society, as so many modern mentalities 'lean away' from duty, logic and conformism. People with a bent middle finger have a somewhat skewed sense of values and hate being called conventional. Invariably they will feel aggrieved by bureaucracy and convention and support the underdog, resenting the workings of 'the system'. They want to avoid seriousness and dislike such values as service and duty, though they're often unsure where their absolute faith lies.

The finger is long when over half the top phalange is proud of the neighbouring digits so that the complete fingernail protrudes clearly above them from the back of the hand. This lends systemised knowledge and great respect for one's chosen authority or value system. Their knowledge tends to the detailed, methodical and practical, though there can be a rather dull pedantry. Often there's a love of history and tradition. You'll find this a common sign on academics, scientists and administrators and people who work within a hierarchy, bureaucracy or system. Such people are wonderful at being dutiful, following instructions and procedures or conforming to arcane regulations; detailed maps or DIY instruction manuals cause them little concern.

When short, the bearers find themselves frustrated by rules and restrictions and they're much more likely to 'opt out' of society. This can be a sign of a potentially disorganised, stressful personality with few personal barriers, unable to accept limitations and, indeed, unable to accept society the way it is. People with short 'wall' fingers are unstable, lacking mental ballast, and they change their values easily. They tend to move around a lot, rarely ever really growing up or settling down.

To mentally wear restriction and convention lightly can be a positive, however, and this is very common on inventive and creative individuals and all sorts of

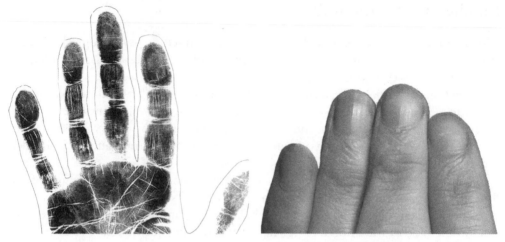

Illustration 47 Long 'wall' digit   *Illustration 48 Short 'wall' digit*

anarchic media types, innovators and sports people who break through to new vistas, pushing back the walls of convention. Also, it's common on restless travellers, 'new agers', spiritual seekers and criminals.

The short 'wall' digit is particularly common on those who live away from, and have little loyalty to, their native country.

Ring finger – peacock's feather

This digit is concerned with the persona, the public face, the pleasure principle and artistic and sporting expression. When long in relation to the index digit on males, it's been linked in several research papers to sporting prowess, virility, a tendency for risk taking and heightened spatial awareness, triggered through high testosterone level exposure in the womb. (Manning J. 'The ratio of 2nd to 4th digit length and performance' *Journal of Sports Medicine and Physical Fitness*, December 2002.)

The ultimate meaning of this digit though is that it's an elaboration of the display and rutting instinct in the competition to attract a mate, hence its peacock feather metaphor.

It's related to all aspects of the drive to display – dressing up, the development of skills, aesthetics, creativity, sports abilities, the pursuit of thrills, danger and distraction. It's also connected with hobbies, entertainment and sense of play.

It's measure is by comparison with the index finger. 78% of men and 62% of women have this digit slightly longer than the index, thus this drive eclipses the self-absorbed processes of the index finger in most of us. If it's no more than half a centimetre longer than the index, this can be dismissed as average.

When the peacock's feather digit is significantly over-developed (a centimetre or more longer than the index) it is invariably on a male hand, as it is far more commonly seen on men.

When long, the need for self-expression, social kudos and the sense of drama is strong; levity tempers self-absorption and one tends not to take oneself too seriously (at least publicly). One seeks expression, appreciation, stimulus and the public stage.

Without doubt, having this finger long offers the potential for greater success in initially attracting a mate, but it's no guide to long-term relationships. Long ring fingers are found on leaders in the more risky, pack-instinct, showy, male-dominated professions, e.g. army captain, venture capitalism, politics, football.

Long ring fingers tend, to some extent, to trust to luck and can put their private selves to one side. Long *index* fingers, however, never really forget themselves; they are unable to hide behind a mask.

People in the public eye, showbiz types, sports people, salespeople, artists, those with a reputation, enigmatic leaders, people who dress for effect – all have ring fingers of exaggerated length. However, they live more in their public lives than private and the sheer willingness to take risks and sense of self-abandon drives success.

Where the ring finger is more than a centimetre longer than the index finger, a certain bravado in the personality masks deep-seated feelings of inadequacy. Such people have a massive difference between public performance and private self-value.

Where the ring finger is very long, the index very short, and no skills, qualities or abilities to 'show off' with are developed, self-destructive behaviour can be present. This is often through all forms of risk taking, be it in gambling or bungee jumping. A pathological need for attention can manifest as a plastic-breasted porn star or a motorcycle stunt rider. All have excessively long ring fingers and will deflect self-analysis with humour if possible.

Very long ring fingers need recognition and often have lots of natural charisma, love dressing up and are natural 'personalities'; but they can certainly be superficial. 'Look at me mummy!' is the obvious childhood refrain thronging through adulthood. They are often born of large families or they had to perform or play up in some way to get attention as a child.

Look at the hands of celebrities: watch their prominent peacock feather digits endure any humiliation for publicity, while their diminutive private self of the mirror digit remains bent and tucked away.

When this digit bends towards the middle finger, the sense of creative expression and pleasure is inhibited by the serious concerns of duty, work and family. A certain martyrdom is evident; they can allow an oppressive sense of obligation to inhibit their happiness.

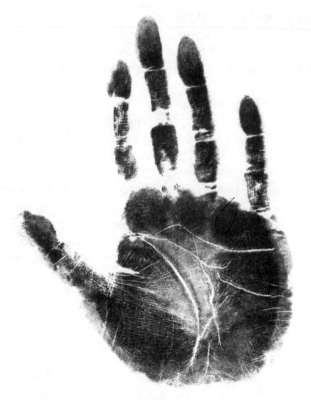

Illustration 49 The hand of a world famous comedian – note the huge ring and tiny index digits

Little finger – the antenna

This digit takes the 'antenna' metaphor as it's concerned with communication at all levels – verbal, signal and sexual, articulation and the neuro-linguistic facility. The average length is for the tip to be level with the top phalange crease of the neighbouring digit. On around one third of women and one tenth of men, it's low set, so that it may look short, but may actually be of average length. Check this by observing the first phalange crease (nearest the palm) of the little finger – it should reach around half way up the base phalange of the ring digit.

When this digit is long, like an extended antenna, it picks up the subtle subtext of language and inference. Its length lends a feel for, and love of, language itself, a natural eloquence and wit, sexual curiosity and a certain physical articulacy. A long finger will naturally pick up and manipulate ideas easily, be they in the field of business, education, finance or comedy and have an innate curiosity and large vocabulary. A long finger is invariably found on, amongst others, politicians, comedians, financial speculators, writers, teachers, sales reps and lawyers.

Illustration 50 A long antenna digit on the hand of a writer

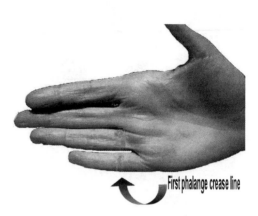

First phalange crease line

Illustration 51 A low set antenna finger

When the digit is low set, its first phalange crease is roughly in line with the base of the ring finger rather then higher up as in the average position.

It's particularly common for women to bear this sign – it's found on around 28% of women's hands. It shows a deep-set underdevelopment in sexual and intimate articulacy. It's connected with the father relationship and signals difficulty in individual expression of the deepest private desires and sexuality. This sign is practically always found where there has been some form of absent father, an extremely close father bond in a sort of 'daddy's girl' role, or sexual abuse. This should never be assumed or made clear, however, as the actual cause may be more obscure. This sign always indicates a drive to surrender one's deeper drives to another's.

Until this feature is understood, there can be sexual immaturity and consequent negative relationship cycles where perfectly strong, capable people surrender themselves to more manipulative or dominant or simply inappropriate partners. It frequently occurs on women who seek a 'father figure' as a partner and those who confuse sex with love. The low-set antenna digit is endemic in the sex industry.

Where this finger is *short*, particularly if it's also low set, as with a small antenna, signals will be missed and communication can be somewhat basic. Often the bearers of weak antenna digits are poor with money. There's usually hostility to wordiness, sarcasm and irony. Such people often lack curiosity, rarely read and have little verbal confidence. They need lots of encouragement to develop verbal dexterity and general acuteness.

If this digit bends towards the ring finger it is traditionally the sign of a liar, but the reality is more complex and subtle than this. Bending towards the display digit gives the quality of tact and the ability to manipulate language for effect, without necessarily expressing the unvarnished truth. It can mean a mimic, a tendency to exaggerate or a penchant for diplomacy, or of saying what others want to hear.

Illustration 52 Missing antenna finger crease

When the digit is very bent, speech is usually inhibited or clichéd to some particular context, e.g. legalese or jargon.

Very occasionally, the finger hasn't developed correctly and the central phalange crease is missing. This is a sign of learning difficulties and difficulty in organising thought; it's very common in Down's Syndrome.

Sometimes this finger naturally sticks out away from the other digits, this indicates eccentricity, and mental and sexual adventurousness: the person who'll study Bantu or wear a stuffed racoon on his head at the office party. On the passive hand, this sign can indicate a sense of isolation.

A standard length, straight finger here can be dismissed as fine and average.

Details, details – knots, fingertips, phalanges

One can make further observations of the fingers by examining the phalanges, the wearing of rings, the shape of the fingertips and the development of knots. Much of this will be irrelevant in a reading as, in most cases, no phalanges stand out disproportionately, there are no rings (apart from a wedding ring), the fingertips are average and the knots aren't particularly well developed. Such features are worthy of study though, as they are very telling and allow you to glean information about a person from a distance.

Rings

Wearing rings on the fingers has the effect of supporting that finger, indicating its importance in the person's life. As readers, we should always be drawn to the digit they're worn on, as a subconscious need for an extra boost or reinforcement in the area indicated. Even if the ring was 'the only finger it would fit on' or was 'inherited from great Auntie Agatha', it seems to 'ring true' to certain inner traits.

The wearing of a ring on the index (mirror) digit denotes self-obsession, a need to dominate or an inferiority complex.

People who require stability and order, who need a sense of values or are concerned with family, money and material things wear a ring on the middle (wall) finger.

A wedding or engagement ring on the ring (peacock's feather) digit displays success in the mating stakes. Other rings here signal someone concerned with their image; performers of all kinds very often wear a ring on this finger.

It's enormously common for sexually available or sexually curious people to wear a ring on the little (antenna) finger; also those who are concerned with communication, e.g. writers, public speakers.

To wear a ring on the thumb shows a desire for greater willpower, inner strength and energy to cope.

In general, a lot of rings on both hands indicate an insecure and troubled personality. This is very common on adolescents when they're establishing themselves in the adult world and on people who feel alienated in some way.

Phalanges

The fingers may occasionally have a complete set of phalanges that stand out by being extra-large or particularly small.

If a level of phalanges stands out on the digits as over or undersized, it's important because it indicates a person who either dwells in or avoids a particular mental realm.

The lower phalanges (nearest the palm) are the sensual realm (the feel, taste and substance of phenomena), the middle phalanges are the executive level (organising, practising and acting out impulses) and the top phalanges are the more abstract realm of thought (appearance, philosophy, projected ideas).

So if (as in the illustration) the base phalanges are all disproportionately large, ideas of a sensual, physical and material nature are naturally exaggerated in the persons mind.

In a similar vein, when one phalange level is particularly *underdeveloped*, the person lacks awareness in that area.

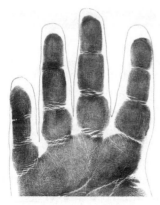

Illustration 53 This lady is a chef, masseuse, self-confessed hedonist and 'chocoholic'

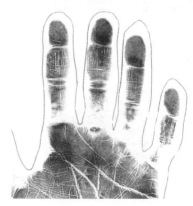

Illustration 54 Small top phalanges

Where the top phalanges are particularly small the person has little interest in the intangible and philosophical and can't understand others who do, the attitude is: 'life's for getting on with, not wondering over'.

Where the middle level phalanges are particularly large, the person will be extremely active and the application, organisation and execution of ideas will dominate their mentality. Where the highest phalanges are overlarge, the person will dwell in the abstract and speculative but won't necessarily put ideas into practice.

Particularly small lower phalanges denote an ascetic. A weak mid-level indicates a poor grasp of organisation and application.

Knots

In traditional palmistry, knots have been known as 'knots of order' or 'knots of argument'. Most people have fairly well developed knots at the first finger joints (closest to the palm), and barely noticeable ones at the second (nearer the fingertip) joints. Hence, only the unusual cases of well-developed *second* joints are significant.

Knots slow down and 'bounce' the mental energy. Where the upper knots are well developed, the subject will be meticulous and thorough, loving to analyse, argue and discuss. They are likely to be sceptical and to understand only what can be worked out through logic and well argued reason. Often, there's a good memory for the oblique, for example: names of obscure pop groups, odd facts or specialist information.

Where the fingers are particularly smooth, there is less mental processing going on and a more spontaneous, intuitive cognition takes place. This is common on physical performers, artistic and expressive types who make mental leaps but have no time for analysis or details.

Fingertips

The fingertips can generally be ignored if most of them are of the common, rounded pattern (see illustration) or if one or two are mildly spatulate. However, sometimes most of the fingertips are squared off, pointed or very spatulate, and this is significant.

The tips themselves are where the mental energy is expressed.

Common, rounded fingertips can safely be dismissed as average.

Pointed fingertips are like arrowheads, flying into clouds of dreamy, far

Illustration 55 Common, rounded fingertip

Illustration 56 Pointed fingertip   *Illustration 57 Squared-off fingertip*

off worlds; they add a romantic aspect to the mind view. A full set, though, can be somewhat unworldly and unrealistic.

When the tip is squared-off, it indicates an ordered and pragmatic mental framework. Everything is labelled, registered and assigned its particular place. It's common on record keepers, sticklers for routine and those in the financial and scientific worlds.

Illustration 58 Spatulate fingertip

The spatulate tip broadens out at the end and is best imagined as bursting with inner force. When found on most of the tips they add a 'get stuck in' attitude to even the most passive of hands. Sets of these are common on sporty types, people with manual and technical skills and active, busy people.

EXERCISE

Now you've got work to do! You can now discern an enormous fund of information about a person's psychology through their fingers. Look for examples of long and short index fingers; long and short middle fingers; long and short ring fingers; low set, long and short little fingers and take prints of them. Annotate the prints you take with an arrow pointing up above a digit that's extra long and an arrow pointing down for a digit that's extra short. Test the flexibility of the fingers by bending them back gently and write a number on your prints from 1 to 5 for how collectively flexible the digits are. Write 3 for average, 5 for extremely floppy, 1 if they're rigidly immobile, 2 for fairly stiff and 4 for fairly flexible. Ask people about their family background, how they feel about themselves, their values, self-expression and communication. Compare their responses with their relative finger lengths and note their responses in your journal.

6

The Biometric Blueprint – Finger and Palm Prints

We'll finish off the fixed, genetic (or karmic) qualities by looking at the finger and palmer prints. These are known as the dermatoglyphics (Latin: derma (skin), glyph (markings)) and are powerful indicators of the prevailing mental 'current' of whatever aspect of personality they're found on. The prints are extremely important, some readers will only examine these in a reading. We'll need to re-visit the digits and thumbs after this chapter in the light of our discoveries and check the prints on them. A small point, like a whorl print in the Lunar quadrant or a radial loop on the 'mirror' finger, has huge consequences, so it's crucial to be patient and examine the hand carefully.

In hand reading, much lies in the details. A good reader is like a detective, examining and sifting the evidence, seeing in the smallest clue a wealth of information.

Before we go on to look at the meaning of a particular dermatoglyphic on a specific area, let's look at their overall form and meaning. This will deepen your understanding of the way they affect consciousness and help your interpretations. Whether on digit or palm, they're potent character markers. In traditional Hindu palmistry, print patterns indicate the flow of karmic forces acting on the person.

Think of the pattern of the dermatoglyphics as replicating the arrangements of the brain's synapses in a given area, shaping the prevailing psychological pattern there.

Once these patterns are explained to and understood by the bearer, they can be moderated against and accepted. Thus, rather than making a client feel trapped in some karmic force, you can set them free. Any disposition, once assimilated and embraced, tends to be a liberating experience.

First, let's take a look at the basic print patterns. Of course, every print pattern on every person is unique, but we can arrange them into five basic patterns as illustrated on the following page.

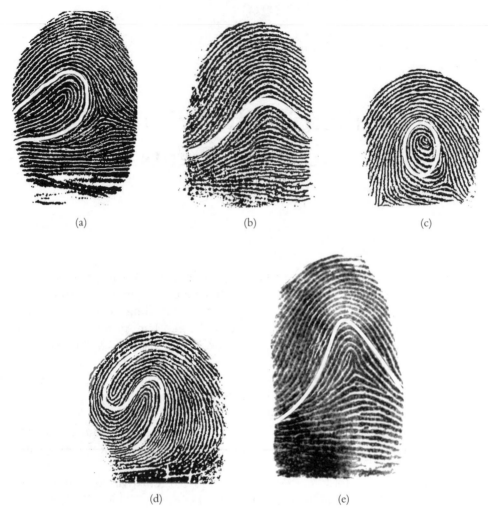

*Illustration 59 The full range of print patterns: (a) loop, (b) simple arch,
(c) whorl, (d) composite, (e) tented arch*

Tented arches and simple arches look alike but the difference is that tented arches are more steeply pitched with a small triradius (pronounced try-ray-dee-us – a node of lines like a tiny three-way junction) pattern in the centre.

Loops on the fingers can be either ulnar (very common) or radial (fairly rare). The difference between these loops is that radial loops open towards the thumb, whereas ulnar loops open towards the little finger.

If we arrange the print patterns into a kind of gradient of movement in a sea of cosmic energy, the simple arches would form the sea bed as these chevron shapes restrict flow, holding energy in, and form a sort of fixing process, while loops represent the main flow or current of energy; tented arches with their sharply angled, spike-like patterns are excitable waves of motion on the ocean's surface.

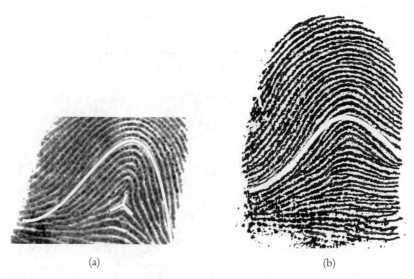

(a) (b)

Illustration 60 (a) Tented arch and (b) simple arch: comparison of the centre of a tented arch with the centre of a simple arch

The composites are like whirlpools of confused eddying current, radial loops are pushed and manipulated by the pressure of the tide and whorl prints are like bubbles of air moving freely in their own direction.

The more there are of a pattern on the digits, the more potent is the prevailing mind–set.

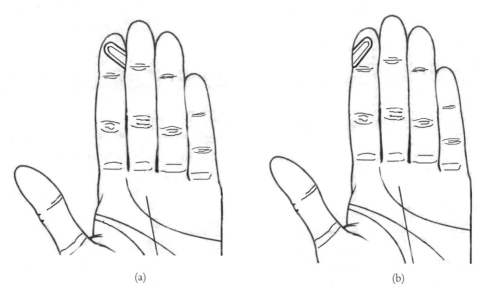

(a) (b)

Illustration 61 (a) Ulnar and (b) radial loops

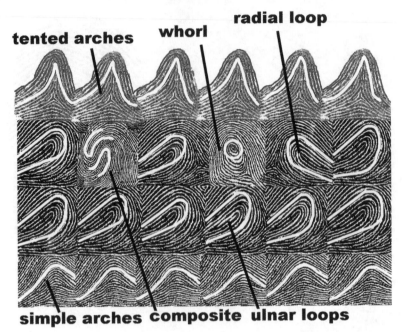

Illustration 62 The cosmic sea

Holistic meaning of the print patterns

Tented arches

These are like splashing wave crests, giving the impulse to break out of boundaries, to be prominent, an excess of enthusiasm and excitement, agitation, restlessness, self-expression, action, a zealot or fanatic, an intense response, impulsive, extreme (these are rare patterns – one is rare on palm or digit, more than one is rare indeed).

Composite

Turbulence, an eddy or whirlpool creating psychological cycles of enthusiasm and disappointment, to be for and against, to go both ways, moodiness, mentally never more than 60% certainty on any point, an openness to explore options, an anti-fanatic, universal viewpoint.

Ulnar loop

By far the most common pattern on palm and digit– the tidal stream, giving an attitude of moving with the current – a sense of empathy, of going with the social flow, gregarious, friendships and relationships are prioritised, adapt easily within conventions, emotive, a feeling response, receptive and impressionable, a need to belong (if this pattern is on all ten digits, it can create an unstable, artistic, responsive personality lacking concentration and needful of boundaries – with poor quality lines it can produce an emotionally compulsive or physically addictive personality).

Radial loop

These give a sense of being trapped and moved by the current, and by the needs of others, a sense of being pushed, shaped and undermined by people, open to exterior stimuli, a compulsion to prioritise others' needs over one's own, insecure, unstable, caring, responsive.

Whorl

Like an existential bubble of air floating freely, giving a sense of not belonging, involved in one's own processes, isolation, a sense of needing space and freedom, original, not connected, different. If there are more than three whorls on the fingers or one whorl pattern on the palm, there's distinct oddness, alienation, individualism, energetic, talented, original, non-mainstream, intense, a need to have one's own world to inhabit, stressful, secretive and a highly motivated person. One who questions everything.

Simple arch

The bedrock, binding and holding, giving the quality of being deep, fixed, materialistic, stubborn, loyal, repressed, prizing equality and faithfulness. A sense of inhibition, unpretentiousness. One that is physical, persistent and practical.

Lots of these arch patterns (more than three on the fingers) makes one highly resistant to slickness, artifice, superficiality, modernity and change. This gives the need for physical and emotional expression to release deeply repressed impulses, one can be ultra conformist in useful and demanding roles and also (contradictorily), resentful and rebellious, particularly in the form of underground or subversive activity. (Eight or more simple arch prints on the digits is very rare.)

Now that you've got a sense of the general shape and psychological effect of the dermatoglyphics, we'll go through each of the patterns on each of the fingers, then we'll cover the patterns found on the palm.

We'll begin with the print pattern on the index 'mirror' digit, as this is the most important.

Mirror (index) digit's print pattern

The print here has huge implications for the bearer's sense of identity and it shapes the manner of their self-reflection.

Ulnar loop

This is common and merely indicates adaptability and sociability. Anything else is highly significant.

Radial loop

This indicates an innately insecure, hyper-receptive sense of identity. Radial loops here often make a super-friendly person who's open to all. This is a very important sign and needs to be understood by the bearer. It can be a source of difficulty on any hand, but is particularly destabilising on a bendy-thumbed hand with weak lines. The loop turned outwards absorbs everything from outside and they are in danger of defining themselves only in response to other people. Criticism can be devastating for bearers of this sign, but when given the support and praise they crave they can achieve much. Being so receptive means they can 'tune in' intuitively to others. On a thick-skinned or long index-fingered hand this can create a defensive person who feels constantly 'under attack'. They internalise others' needs as their own and can be guilty of being what others want, rather than what they themselves are. Their sensitivity makes for a good carer, therapist or people person, but advice should always be given to spend more time alone and develop self-knowledge.

Whorl

This gives a strong sense of individualism, a tendency to single-mindedness and non-conformism. Whorled-index fingered people need lots of space and won't like being ordered around. It signals originality, a strong sense of individuality and the need to work everything out for themselves. Usually there's a certain degree of secrecy. They always need to create their own niche in life where they can follow their own paths unhindered. It's very common on the self-employed.

Simple arch

This gives a solid, unpretentious shape to the personality. Security and stability are important, though they may too easily place restrictions on their own potentials for change and get trapped in cycles. Confidence may develop very slowly. There's a dogged, dependable quality here, a pragmatist with a somewhat emotionally repressive, cautious tendency.

Tented arch (rare)

This gives a dynamic intensity and edgy nervousness to the personality. Bearers of this sign want excitement and extreme experiences, they want to change the world. It's common on people who are a touch 'over the top' and on those who teach, entertain or motivate others. Usually they're particularly lively souls. Such people need both excitement and to learn how to relax.

Composite (rare)

This gives a somewhat spilt sense of identity. Here one is presented with a duality in self-perception and consequent inner conflict. A vacillating self-image makes personal decisions difficult and can undermine confidence to an alarming degree. Life decisions are often left to the demands of the situation or others' needs rather than what one actually wants. They need to live a varied life, living out two separate sides of character rather than find a fixed role. There's a gift for impartiality and diplomacy; they excel in any situation requiring arbitration or conciliation.

The thumb's print pattern

Now we'll explore the second most important print location – that on the thumb. In this case, the print pattern governs the prevailing attitude to wilful endeavour. On many thumbs, the print is the *only* discerning feature.

The thumb is subject to less variety of patterns than the rest of the digits.

Loops

Loops are the most common pattern found here (nearly two thirds of thumbs bear this pattern), hence this must be regarded as normal and can be safely ignored. It indicates a cooperative, flexible and variable attitude to one's endeavours.

Whorls

Whorl patterns on the thumb indicate a self-motivated attitude, someone headstrong who'll do things their own way and brush opposition aside. There's a love of innovation and originality, they tend to trust their own experience over the expertise of others. Whorl-thumbed love to show off their independence and go it alone.

Simple arches

Simple arch prints signal a stubborn, practical streak, someone who'll take on endeavours to pragmatic and financial ends. Not necessarily an innovator in approach, but very thorough and persistent.

Double loop composites

Double loop composites here can destabilise someone with an otherwise well-appointed thumb unless this is understood. The diverging currents indicate an inconsistent, vacillating attitude to endeavours. They can have difficulty in seeing a course of action through. They tend be moody and alternate between enthusiasm and great doubt. Indecision is the obvious interpretation. It's hard to be decisive with such a pattern, but it adds a considered, multi-viewed outlook that is always conciliatory. Bearers of this marking never mind if a plan is abandoned, they see the benefits and disadvantages of all possibilities.

They should always be counselled to value their ability to see two ways to any goal and to persist though their own inevitable doubts, also advise them that for them to be only 60% certain of anything is enough to go ahead.

The wall (middle) digit's print pattern

Ulnar loop

This is normal and very common so can be ignored. It indicates a varied and flexible approach to values.

Simple Arch

An arch print shapes views on work and belief systems into simple, pragmatic and often somewhat old-fashioned patterns. They have a sense of duty and like order, method and fairness in the values they follow. Justice is particularly important, as is helping others practically. There can be a scientific bent on an Airy hand or a gift for research. The vocational drive is towards a secure, serious, financially rewarding position and a stable lifestyle, rather than one that's exotic. There's usually a fascination with history and ethnicity.

Whorl

Here the values will be highly original with a distinct disregard of dogma and rules. They're likely to have odd or unusual beliefs and lifestyles and be very open minded; extremism is possible if the finger is also short.

A belief in individualism is upheld and they tend to choose freedom over worldly success. There's always either an unusual job or quirky hobby, and their home may be innovative; frequently they'll follow a non-traditional spiritual path.

Composite (rare)

There will inevitably be doubt about where they stand in terms of cultures, spirituality, values and job choice. They suffer continual anxiety about finding the correct career, religion or belief system and question these constantly. As always where there's a composite, a varied and diverse lifestyle is advised, where one can be two things at once, e.g. material and spiritual, insurance broker and artist.

Radial loop (rare)

The sense of cultural identity will be fluid and the person will be able to adapt to different lifestyles and cultures easily. They can be over-conformist or alternative in equal measure and are likely to be one or the other to extreme. They're more than likely to belong to a group of 'Greens' or be religious devotees than most, and more likely to adapt to a foreign culture. They can be overly conscious of their obligations to family and authority.

Peacock's feather (ring) digit's print pattern

Ulnar loop

This print is very common here and indicates a responsiveness to creativity, music, colour and social pleasures, it inclines one to teamwork and a sense of communal enjoyment. It's frequently seen on actresses and creative people who work in teams. This is common enough to be normal.

Whorls

Whorls are common here. They signify originality in creativity, individual taste in dress, music and arts and a desire to stand out. A well-developed sense of perspective with good spatial awareness is assured, with design, visual, and general artistic abilities. If this finger is also long, there will be artistic potentials and an original eye – it's very common on hairdressers, interior decorators, artists and photographers.

Simple Arch (rare)

Here there's a repressive tendency socially. This pattern 'flattens out' the ability to show excitement and really let go. There's a drive to express oneself practically in crafts, through physical activity and in useful and traditional skills – this is often the sign of a talented cook. Usually there's a feeling for natural materials, ethnic art and traditional skills such as weaving or blacksmithery.

Radial loop

This is a rare marker here, giving a hyperawareness of the needs of others, the bearers dislike to see anyone unhappy. They feel pressured to be relentlessly cheerful and to put on a happy social front, loving to make others laugh and hating being a 'party pooper'. They desire to build a reputation socially and need to be noticed. Creatively, they may lack originality or at the very least need to steal ideas and adapt them.

Composites

Composites are practically unknown on this digit.

Antenna (little) digit's print pattern

Ulnar loops

Ulnar loops are nearly always present here. This indicates a flexible, variable communication mode and is the universal norm.

Whorls

Whorl prints are rare on this digit and those with this marking can be relied on to make oblique references and odd observations, with originality in mental perspective generally. They often like unconventional relationships and their sexual patterns tend to be intense, with long periods of abstinence.

There is always a passion for the unusual. They can be drawn to odd love matches and may be very reticent in a crowd, often feeling on another level until their own subject is mentioned when they can be eloquent and obsessive. Often they are storehouses of knowledge of obscure subjects.

Simple arches

Simple arch prints (rare) inhibit speech and mental processing, so they create careful talkers who don't like mental leaps of subject. They may be naturally gifted in sign language and basic exposition. They are deeply reticent about personal intimacy.

Composites and **radial loops** are almost unknown on this digit.

Palmer dermatoglyphics

The loops, whorls, arches and other prints are formed in the woodgrain-like skin ridge patterns, and can be found on the palmer surface as well as on the fingertips.

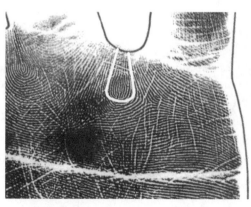

Illustration 63 Loop of leisure

Most hands feature at least one palmer pattern (usually on the lunar quadrant). They are easy to recognise and interpret and, just like on the fingers, they affect the aspect of personal consciousness 'ruled' by that part of the hand.

Loops between digits (illustration 63) 'bind' the qualities of the two fingers together. In this case, the loop is between the 'antenna' and 'peacocks feather' fingers. The 'antenna' digit injects a stream of ideas into the creative expression of the 'peacock' digit. It makes for a sense of fun, wit and levity; such people want enjoyment, can be easily bored and have little long-term capacity for serious careers. Indeed, the professions and purely financially rewarding work rarely attracts where you have one of these loops on each hand. Holidays, travel, hobbies and leisure activity will be crucial in that person's life. It's often found on people in 'fun' professions: actors, musicians, holiday reps. They tend to make a career out of a hobby, be it shiatsu or photography, the priority being fulfilment and stimulation rather than earning power. Even on the most industrious, fiery hand, there's a drive towards early retirement, and the golf course or holiday home constantly beckons.

The 'loop of industry' is the opposite pattern to the above, found between the 'wall' and 'peacock's feather' digits. Here the drive for creativity and stimulation is sublimated into the serious business of work and conformity. This loop indicates that work and duty are a kind of pleasure; they'll be industrious and get the job done. The value of pure leisure is questioned. Material success is prioritised, they'll be business-like and career-minded.

A strong work ethic means that they may well ignore holidays and tend to overwork, so a little self indulgence needs to be encouraged.

The 'loop of leadership' sign is relatively rare and links the sense of self of the 'mirror' digit with the pragmatic, structured 'wall' digit. It gives natural organisational ability and the inclination to acquire status within a group, be it the hen party organiser or the executive sales manager.

The reasonably common 'loop of sensitivity' in the lunar quadrant gives latent sensitivity and possible psychic perception if the skin is fine; certainly an ability to

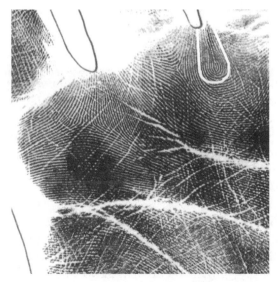
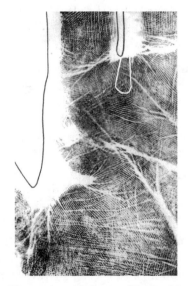

Illustration 64 Loop of industry   *Illustration 65 Loop of leadership*

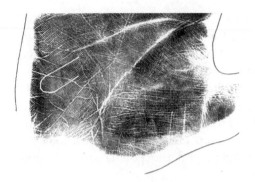
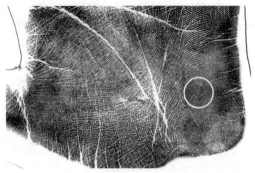

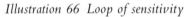

Illustration 66 Loop of sensitivity

Illustration 67 Whorl on the lunar (whorl of isolation)

see deeply into others is present. A sense of *déjà vu*, resonance and general perceptive sensitivity are all emphasised, as are artistic responses; it's much more potent when the Air line ends within the loop.

A whorl on the lunar area, 'the whorl of isolation', energises, activates and cuts off the subconscious lunar area. There's a sort of psychological withdrawal to an inner world and a sense of not completely connecting to others. It's as if the inner life can't be shared or known. People with this sign are self-contained, secretive, hard to really know and, often, a little odd. They have a fascination with psychology, an inventive subconscious, are a touch 'edgy' and can be very artistic. Frequently, there's a desperate need for attention in order to feel connected to others. They usually work alone and can tend to get trapped either within or outside of themselves. Always advise art as therapy for such people.

The triradius

This is a sort of three-way junction of skin ridges that sends a surge of energy through the various patterns. This pattern is found within many print shapes (except for the simple arch). The most important triradius, though, is the one at the centre of the palm base known as the axial triradius.

Its normal placement is at, or very close to, the base of the palm. When placed an inch or more higher than this, or where there's an extra, higher placed triradius, it's particularly significant.

Where this occurs, the bearers have a kind of intensity of pressure inside themselves. There's a geyser-like turbulence within.

This can indicate the possibility of some genetic abnormality and it's very common on people with Down's Syndrome. With this sign there is a greater likelihood of genetic heart weakness. Be wary of mentioning this fact to anyone, as you'll only increase stress levels; simply inform them that they're an intense type who simply *must* have a healthy, stress-free lifestyle.

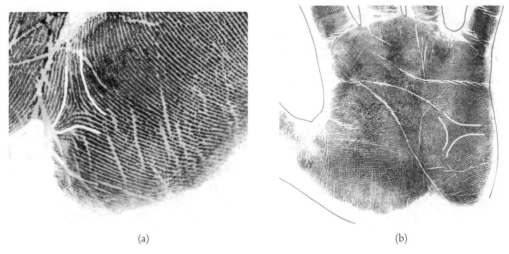

(a)   (b)

Illustration 68 (a) Normal and (b) raised axial triradius

Digital triradii

Triradii are also found around the base of each digit. Sometimes though, the *ring finger* has a kind of necklace of straight lines underneath, with the triradius itself missing. This creates a reluctance to engage the creative and self-expressive drives, they rarely see themselves as artistic. There's a kind of inability to really let go and enjoy themselves and a tendency to depression and irony. They're always aware of the dark side of life.

This pattern is nullified by a fine line crossing the 'collar' and moving towards the finger, indicating a developed sense of fun. Anyone with this 'collar' pattern should always be advised to learn to let go and enjoy life. See illustration 69.

A loop at the side of the lunar quadrant (see illustration 70) opens the area to natural forces. It's a sure sign of receptivity to the earth's energies, a love of nature and an affinity with plants, animals and the countryside. With this sign, even the airiest of hands needs to be near growing things, and on an Earth hand there is often a withdrawal into nature, with a propensity to find cities hellish places.

A very similar loop (illustration 71), but anywhere lower down than that in illustration 70, near the bottom of the Lunar mount, lends a deeper awareness: a sense of what lies beneath the surface of life. This

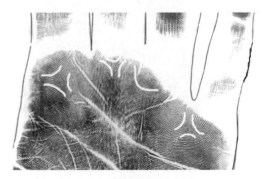

Illustration 69 Missing ring finger triradius

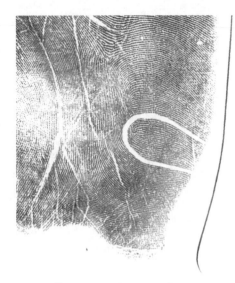
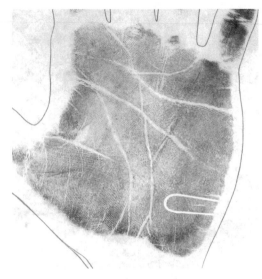

Illustration 70 Loop of nature   *Illustration 71 Loop of mystery*

may mean an interest in mysteries, hidden things, esoteric philosophies, the occult or digging up the past. Both this and the loop of nature can give a gift for dowsing and healing, possibly also a feel for energy points in the body and the Earth.

Rising from the middle of the base of the palm, the 'loop of inspiration' is like a spout of inspiration flowing into the subconscious. It's common on musicians, spiritual seekers and those fascinated by dreams. It gives great power to the capacity of inspiration. Artists often have one of these loops. There's an awareness of deeper levels of life, and a love of the mystical, cosmic, religious and downright strange.

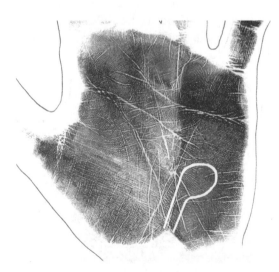

The 'loop of rhythm' is often somewhat squared in shape, raising up from the bottom of the Venus mount. It gives a sense of rhythm and a love of musical harmony. It's not necessarily a sign of musical talent, but bearers will definitely be strongly attracted by music in all its forms, not in a cerebral, but more in a tribal, physical manner. It's very common on dancers and drummers.

A whorl on Venus mount is a rare indication, and would give a need to create a mobile or certainly unconventional household. It's common on people who live in caravans and

Illustration 72 Loop of inspiration

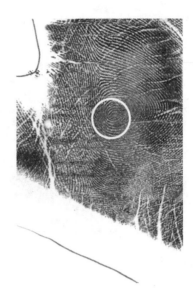

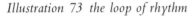

Illustration 73 the loop of rhythm   *Illustration 74 Whorl on Venus mount*

boats, perpetual travellers, those in odd houses; in one of my own examples, I have a woman who built her own house from reeds!

Mars is the god of war, and this lends a great respect for courage and heroism. A loop on the Mars mount is found on those who need to set themselves challenges. On a very physical hand, it may well lead to martial arts skills; on a more passive one, a fascination with ancient battlefields or heroes. Usually, there's a love of sports or, at least, an admiration of heroic struggles and sports people. These folks need to challenge themselves, be it in conquering mountains or fronting a band.

A composite in the Lunar quadrant is a like a whirlpool that constantly churns up the subconscious. The individual can experience great ups and downs emotionally, with mood swings, depression and confusion about what they really feel. They often sense they could love anyone, of either gender. Sometimes they can take on traditionally opposite sex qualities, so that men become passive receptive and women dominant controlling. There can be difficulty in maintaining relationships because of constant instability about what one actually feels for another. Advice to give is that they will always experience a certain amount of inner turmoil, so they should stick to a partner who offers stability above all.

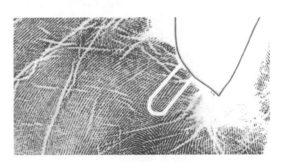

Illustration 75 Loop on Mars mount

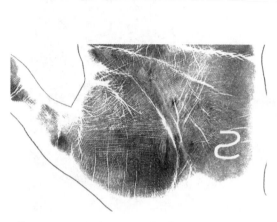 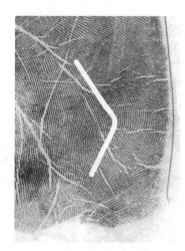

Illustration 76 Composite in the Lunar quadrant   *Illustration 77 Arch on Lunar quadrant*

The study of gender, sexuality and psychology are often areas of expertise. This sign has been linked to sex chromosome disorders.

An arch on the Lunar quadrant indicates emotional reticence and general inhibition. There's usually a reluctance to dress in any way considered inappropriate and to really express their inner drives. They must be encouraged to let off steam physically. It's common on midwives, masseurs and carers. They connect to others by practically demonstrating their affections.

EXERCISE

You're now able to develop very specific and penetrating insights into anyone's personality and potentials; all of their fixed dispositions have now been covered.

As the features we've looked at so far don't change, the qualities uncovered will always be present and are therefore particularly important and powerful.

Study this dermatoglyphic section every day for a week until you have a good idea of their meanings. Read through some of the prints in your collection and check the print patterns you find. Now read your own hand and work out all your fixed patterns (shape, skin texture, thumb and digit qualities, dermatoglyphics) paying particular attention to the differences between the active and passive hands.

Make sure you've assimilated all that we've covered so far before you go to the next chapter – try to get a print of every type of palmer dermatoglyphic.

7

On the Right Lines –
the Major Lines

Now we move on to the non-fixed palmer features: the highly individual and changeable lines of the hand. Many people assume reading the lines is all palmistry consists of, understanding little of all the other points one must take into consideration. The lines mean little outside the context of the hand they're situated on.

In this chapter, we'll establish what the lines actually mean and study their underlying principles. Then we'll go on to interpret two of the four major lines using their reading metaphors.

The lines are rivers of energy, or *chi*, moving through various organs and areas of consciousness. Each main line has an elementary quality, which reflects a particular form of energetic current within the person.

The lines form between the ninth and eleventh weeks of gestation and change slowly and subtly throughout one's lifetime. Consequently, it's advisable to take prints annually and to re-read for people as their patterns change.

If the hand shape, skin texture, prints and fingers form the unchanging potentials of a person, the lines are the individual expression of that potential. A long, clear Air (head) line on a long-fingered, silk-skinned, hand means one thing, and a long clear Air (head) line on a short-fingered hand with coarse skin means something else. The former may be a literary agent, while the latter may be a mechanical engineer. One inhabits the conceptual milieu, while the other inhabits the solid, material world. The lines are always read against the background of what you know already, through the previous frames of the permanent patterns.

There are four major lines and these are usually present in some rudimentary form in everyone.

There are also usually, but by no means necessarily, other minor lines present.

A few principles are worth remembering to make it easy to interpret and understand the lines.

The flow of the lines should ideally be like that of a free-flowing river, unimpeded by islands, blocks and breaks. In this respect, a very thick, trench-like line is similar to a silted-up river; and a faint, striated line is like a very shallow

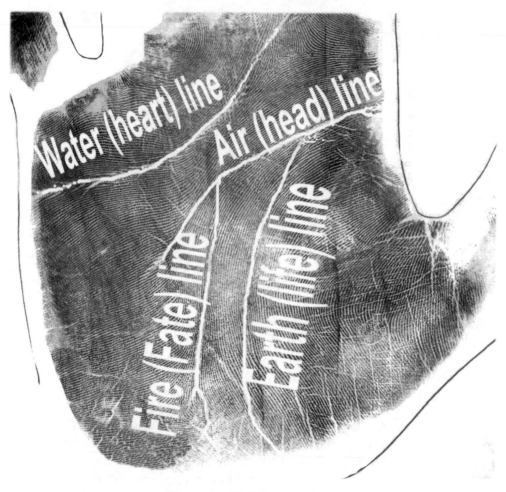

Illustration 78 The major lines

brook. In either case, the flow and function of the line will be poor. Straight red lines are strong torrents of energy, very direct and perhaps unsubtle, where curved, faint lines are more delicate and considered.

The major lines should be roughly balanced in strength. If any line stands out as substantially stronger, this should ideally be the Earth line. If not, the person currently 'dwells' too much in some non-physical aspect of themselves and their lives will be somewhat out of balance. For instance, if the Water (heart) line is very strong and deep, while all the other lines are fainter (see illustration 114 for an example of this), then physical energy and stability (Earth line), goals (Fire line) and mental clarity (Air line) are currently at the mercy of the emotional state (this is very common on someone undergoing a divorce or suffering a recent bereavement).

Lines can also be too long or too short. If a major line crosses the palm from side to side or top to bottom, this creates a compulsion of some sort. If a line's very short, a person will have a limited range in that area.

The lines are influenced by the area of the palm they're on and the digit they point towards.

Like the palmer and finger prints, the lines are unique – no two people have exactly the same lines (even twins). Moreover, everyone assumes that we all see and experience the world similarly to themselves. It can be a shock to discover how much we vary in the way we interpret the exterior world.

Lines record the *individual's* interpretation of events. This is a big idea to swallow but, ultimately, it means there's no absolute objective truth out there. For instance, two children in the same family can experience the divorce of their parents differently and record the experience differently in their hands.

A fascinating aspect of the lines is that they reflect their characteristics both momentarily and chronologically. This is to say that a bar, break or island on a line is indicative not only of an event occurring at a particular *time* in the bearer's life, but also there's a moment-to-moment blip in their consciousness *presently*.

For example: a large island at the end of the Air line reflects not only a stressful and incoherent mental process in the latter years of the bearer's life (this often signifies age-induced dementia) but this sign also indicates stress and incoherence in the way they formulate concepts and express themselves *currently*.

As a general principle, the higher the marking physically on the palm itself, the more idealised and abstract is the energy moving within the line and the more it relates to higher functions and higher parts of the body. For example: a line above the Water line, near the fingers, is linked to fantasy and escapism and is associated with the head physically. Small lines here often indicate a tendency to experience migraine attacks.

The base of the Earth line at the bottom of the palm relates to the sense of place and grounding and, physically, to the sphincter.

Lines or branches of lines that reach upwards towards the fingers are expressive of optimism, idealism and positive attitudes and events.

Lines that plunge downwards are linked to a sense of 'holding on', depression, loss, draining energy and negative events.

A break in a line shows an interruption in a person's life. If the two parts of the line overlap, they'll move quickly into new experiences; if there's a large gap with no overlap, they'll ceases to function in the area represented by the line and, for the period of the gap, they'll be particularly vulnerable to breakdown and illness. Always check the quality of a line *after* a break. If the line becomes clearer, the experience will eventually prove beneficial.

Islands in a line indicate an inability to cope with a situation, confusion and stress.

Forked lines indicate diversity. Often one branch is stronger and this is the dominant pattern.

Little bar lines cutting across important lines represent exterior obstacles.

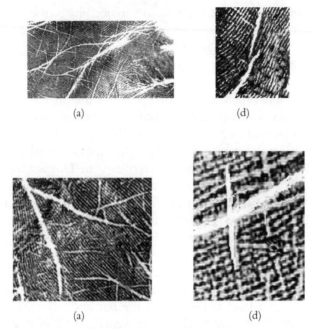

(a)   (d)

(a)   (d)

Illustration 79 (a) Island, (b) break, (c) fork, (d) bar line

Where there are an enormous number of lines all over the hand, there's mental hyperactivity, lots of fleeting responses and impressions, and, just possibly, neurosis. This is known as a 'full hand'. Such a person would be highly-strung, complex and sophisticated but easily overloaded, stressed and liable to exhaustion. This is more likely on long-fingered hands with fine skin.

Where there are very few lines on the palm, the personality lacks complexity. They're focused within mental boundaries and both concrete and certain about what they know. They like to be direct and unambiguous, plain and straightforward in dress, manner and thinking. Having few lines isn't necessarily a sign of lack of sensitivity though, only if the skin quality is also coarse.

Where the palm is very broad, the skin coarse, the fingers short and only very thick, basic lines

Illustration 80 A 'full' hand

present, there's the possibility of a lack of refinement, slow mental responses and learning difficulties, as if the person isn't quite 'switched on'.

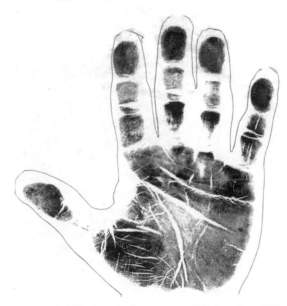

Illustration 81 The hand of a person with learning difficulties

Each line is best understood through its interpretative metaphor.

Earth line (lifeline)

One of the unfortunate legacies of traditional, predictive palmistry is that most laymen are aware of the old nonsense about a short or broken lifeline presaging an early demise!

The way to think of this line is as a *root*. It embeds itself into the base of the palm, creating stability for the branches of personality (represented by the other main lines) to thrive and express themselves; drawing energy (chi), nourishment and vitality into the body, establishing a sense of security.

Strong, clear, semi-circular roots create strong physical rhythms of circulating energy – the repetitive patterns of eating, sleeping and digestion; giving one's life rhythm; a cycle of vitality running through the whole span of the day, the year, the lifetime.

Our roots are, of course, our family and our sense of place. On the passive hand, a break in this line indicates a major disturbance in upbringing. Usually this is parental divorce, a major move, loss of a parent or sibling, or some other severe shock to stability.

Where the *base* of the Earth line is missing or broken off on the passive hand, it's because the family was uprooted or changed cultures. It's very common on first generation immigrants and the children of highly mobile or unstable parents. Someone with a missing base section finds it hard to feel stable and rooted.

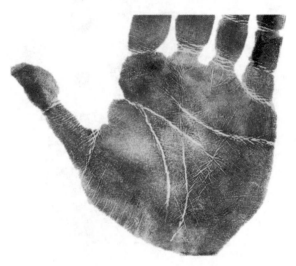

Illustration 82 Earth line with missing base section

If the Earth lines on both hands are deep, clear and complete, one is able to stand on one's own two feet and thrive anywhere. Such roots deliver abundant nutrients and energy, and one feels well-grounded with a sense of place, good digestion and internal stability.

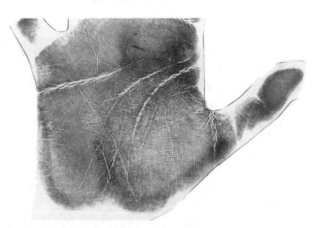

Illustration 83 Short, weak Earth line

If the Earth line is short and feeble, the bearer will have weak assimilation of food and be ungrounded; there'll be insecurity, poor energy, uncertain health, no pattern to diet, activity or sleep; they'll lack a sense of permanence.

A weak Earth line isn't itself a sure sign of poor health *per se*, but an indication of fragility and a weak grip on life, like a weak-rooted plant.

Such people will need security from *outside* themselves, usually in the form of a steady partner, material wealth or secure career to keep stable. In the same way a weak shoot will cling to the trunk of an oak for support. They can be vulnerable to cults, chaotic and unstable life patterns, domineering partners and sudden changes of fortune.

If such a sign is on both hands, they'd have no idea what a sense of internal calm and stability is like; family life always was and currently is chaotic with no rhythm; they're apt to feel easily threatened and unsure of their ground. Crucially, they can't create stability and support themselves.

Having and raising one's own children, or establishing a stable home life and physical routine, strengthens a weak Earth line very quickly.

The natural shape of this line is a semi-circle. If the line sweeps well out into the centre of the palm, it shows abundance and vitality, the drive to get stuck into life. If it remains close to the thumb, it indicates timidity and restraint.

Sometimes the line begins very high up, near the base of the index finger. This shows an ambitious, striving nature, particularly if there are little lines shooting upward here.

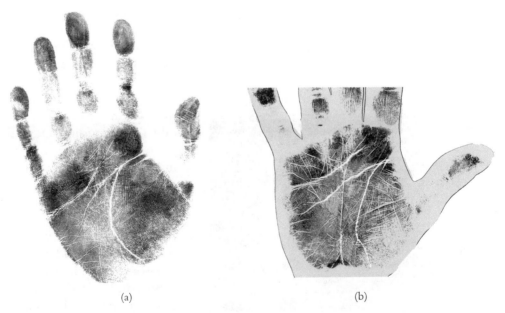

(a)   (b)

Illustration 84 Earth lines with (a) wide sweep, (b) set close to thumb and
high set

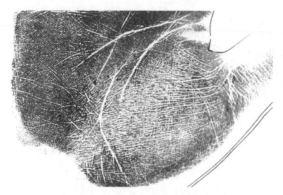

Illustration 85 The Earth line breaks here and renews itself further out towards the centre of the palm. This is someone who divorced, started a career and began a more adventurous life

Breaks in the Earth line on the active hand show seismic shifts in one's lifestyle, which incur a fresh start, like replanting one's whole life: divorce, major illness, crucial relocation – any or all these important life shifts.

Look at the condition of the line *after* the break – if it's stronger, they'll thrive, if it's weaker, there'll be problems; advise a healthy regimen be established.

If the new section of the line jumps further out towards the centre of the palm, they'll live a fuller life, usually developing a new career; if it's closer to the thumb, they'll live a more enclosed, quieter life than previously.

Note that a divorce may not show here, particularly if it was relatively amicable and no house move occurred. Breaks and renewed lines often point to times when people change weight, hairstyle – everything about themselves, though sometimes the change is more internalised.

An Earth line that's striated (this is when the line is made of fine broken lines) shows someone unsettled and nervous with poor internal stability. The bearer will be prone to incomplete digestion. They'll find it difficult to commit to anyone or anything and they'll lack stamina. Energy is inconsistent and easily drained – a simple, regular physical routine is always advisable in such cases.

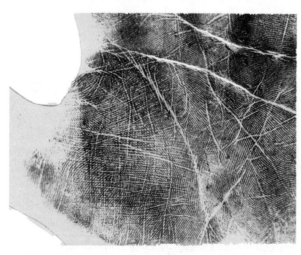

Illustration 86 Striated Earth line

A line made up of islands is similar – like a root saturated with Water it indicates unstable family relationships, weak digestion and poor mineral assimilation; such people love to take frequent baths.

A very thick, trough-like line can indicate high levels of toxicity within the body.

A large single island near the base of the line indicates an unhappy, unstable time in late middle age and possibly illness.

The very base of this line near the wrist is the anchor, showing how fixed in place a person is. When the line curls deep into the thumb ball, the bearer will be strongly fixed with a sense of permanence. Often such folk are unwilling to travel and remain close to their background and family. Where this part of the line is missing (not merely broken off) they can be prone to being transient and not bound to any one place. Invariably they're permanently 'spaced out' and impractical; unable to stick the yoga class or fix the car, but keen to investigate past lives and higher planes.

Branches

Lines branching away at the base of the line indicate a desire for travel and change. On a more Earthy hand, this may merely mean a member of the local ramblers. There's always adventurousness about people with such lines.

A fork here gives both homing instinct and travel urge.

Where you have a curled-in root on the passive hand and a travel line on the active, you have someone who'll make a comfortable home of a caravan or holiday chalet.

If the whole line ends in the lunar quadrant like a root wandering into the next field, the person will be highly mobile and adventurous, always looking to belong. They'll forever search for their roots. For them, life is truly a journey. Such people are very likely to emigrate.

Small lines leading up off the main line reaching towards the Jupiter quadrant show new beginnings, like new shoots of growth. These are positive events –

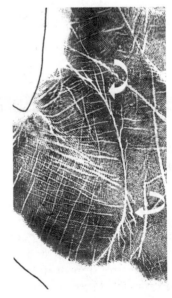

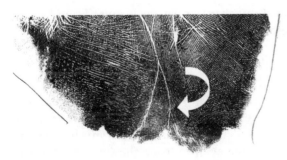

Illustration 87 Travel line on an air steward's hand

Illustration 88 Rising lines from the Earth line and falling lines near the base

new job, diet, child or promotion. Lines dropping off the main line are draining energy, indicating restlessness, the need for change and dissatisfaction.

Markings within the Earth line

Lines that run parallel to and within the main line are supports and structures. There are usually quite a few of these – they're rather like little props that sustain us through life. Long-term friendships, brothers and sisters, husbands, wives and close friends – even pets. Invariably, identical twins have a single, very long line parallel to their Earth line.

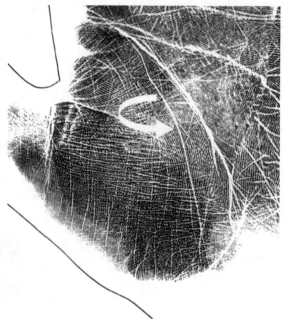

Illustration 89 A support line within the Earth line on the hand of a twin

Usually an abundance of these lines show that the person is quite bound up in the lives of others, and a lack of these indicates the person considers themselves autonomous.

A short, clear line within the base of the Earth line indicates a need to really get away from it all, to retreat to the rural idyll or cabin in the woods late in life.

Lines which cross the whole Jupiter mount are stress lines. They aren't particularly important and most of us have some of these. If there is an abundance of these, it's a sure sign of domestic stress and a chaotic home life. If any line crosses and breaks the Earth line, it tells of a negative event outside the subject's control, but within the domestic sphere – often accidents to self or close ones, financial loss, house subsidence, bankruptcy, all such indications are regrettably negative.

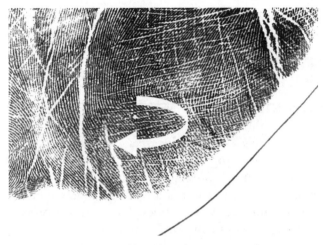

Illustration 90 A 'retreat' line within the lower base of the Earth line

*Illustration 91 Stress line breaking the Earth line – this example was a
near-fatal accident to a partner*

A fascinating irony is that when the Earth line is clear and bold the bearers usually take their good health totally for granted. They're rarely ill so seldom concern themselves with their bodies, which can mean eventual ill health due to neglect.

Complementary therapists (homoeopaths, shiatsu practitioners and the like) tend to have surprisingly *weak* Earth lines. This is because their interest in health comes from an exploration of their own sensitivities and physical weaknesses and the consequent development of alternative strategies to deal with them.

Illustration 83 (the short Earth line) is actually on the hand of a homoeopath.

Though the slowest to change, the Earth line does alter throughout life, and its quality improves enormously with a healthy diet and a simple, stable and rhythmic lifestyle.

Doubled Earth lines

Occasionally this line is found doubled, with two distinct lines. On the passive hand this represents two very different parents and a sense of two separate value systems or cultures. Usually there's a tension between two different early paths to take (university or motherhood, for instance) and early commitments have to be eventually rejected in favour of more adventurous ones.

If the doubling is on the *active* hand, it always gives an abundance of energy and the sense of needing to embrace two lifestyles. There are always two distinct sides to the person's life. On a woman's hand this is invariably the tension between family and career, but here one never reconciles the two – one is a different person in each aspect of life.

The need for two paths in life can mean a very demanding city career and a second life as a country bumpkin; usually there is tremendous travel and movement between the twin bases, roots and lifestyles.

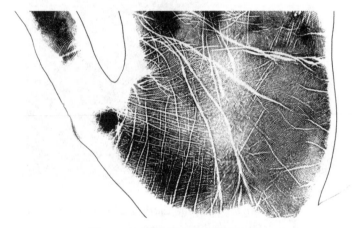

Illustration 92 Doubled Earth lines

Timing

All major lines mark events in a linear, chronological fashion, but the Earth line is the only one measurable with any rough degree of accuracy. The line begins at the top palm edge, between the thumb and index fingers and ends at the base of the thumb ball. Its full length is around eighty-four years. The cycles of time move in seven-year intervals and though this process seems childishly simplistic, with experience one is able to time events on this line with considerable accuracy.

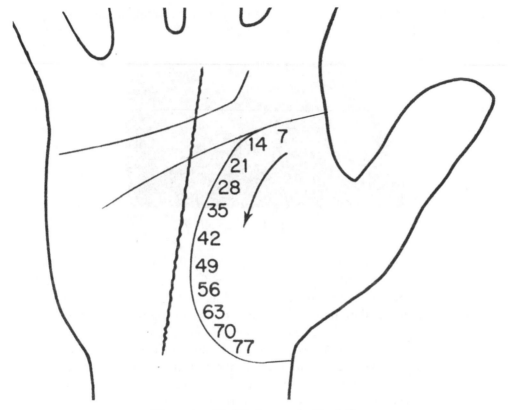

Illustration 93 Timing on the Earth line

Air (head) line

The Air line is the key to a person's personality, as it illustrates the way the person conceives and communicates.

Whether we think independently, logically, symbolically or objectively, is to a great extent what make us ourselves. People with very different Air lines are on different wavelengths, and perceive the world in differing ways.

The metaphor to use for this line is a light beam. Notice how often we use this image for mental qualities – 'she's a bright spark', 'it came in a flash', indeed, we say that gaining wisdom is the process of becoming en*light*ened.

The longer this line extends across the palm, the further mentally one illuminates the darkness of possibilities and the more that is taken into consideration in any decision. Long lines (ending under the antenna finger) take a long view of things.

People with long air lines are philosophically inclined, and think 'outside the box'. For example, in considering a prospective house purchase, they'll take into account the long-term housing market, the possibilities of other houses as yet unexplored, the ethics of materialism and the point of moving at all. They spend a lot of time looking beyond the now, asking 'what if?'.

Illustration 94 A long Air line

A short Air line (ending somewhere under the 'wall' digit) sees a smaller picture, and is more immediate and focused on what's before them. Their minds are like a desk lamp illuminating only what's on the table. In a prospective house purchase they'll consider immediate practicalities, like the new neighbours, the need for an extra bedroom and the price value of the new house.

Contrary to what you might expect, short Air lines (if clear) are more successful than long lines in examinations and in the acquisition of new skills where practical, applied and recalled information is required. They have excellent focus and concentrate on the information at hand without distraction.

Short lines tend to be successful in business and in highly skilled work – they're mentally concentrated on the tangible world. Their limited vision may be a problem when considering the long-term, broader picture; but they're excellent at *applied* ideas.

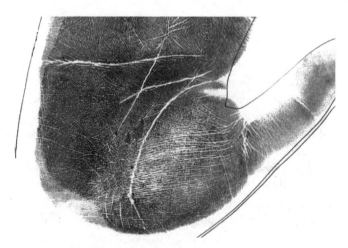

Illustration 95 A short Air line

Long lines are successful in areas such as advising, speculating, instructing, estimating and in such subjects as literature and philosophy; comparing ideas and approaches. They tend to project into the future and make judgements based on how *they* encapsulate things, where a short line rarely expresses a personal view.

Long lines look beyond the immediate to the bigger picture – and often question common assumptions; not so useful in a practical business, but helpful in a consultancy of some kind where an overview is necessary. The average length of the Air line is an ending under the 'peacock feather' digit – this is a good balanced perspective between the immediate and prospective.

Always check the clarity of this line – if the light beam is broken up, full of islands or bar lines, the person can't see clearly. Their mental picture is incoherent. Internally, they're in a mental fog of distraction and confusion. Usually they're found on timid, ineffective people who allow others to think for them.

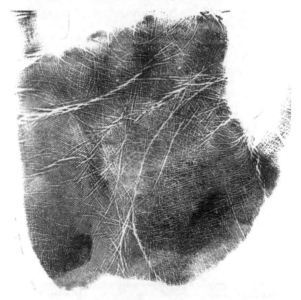

Illustration 96 A poor quality Air line

Islands on the Air line are mentally stressful points where the mind continually distorts issues out of proportion. Check which finger any island (or other marking on any horizontal line) is found under to reveal something of the cause. An island under the index finger relates to problems in self-perception, ambitions and parental expectations; under the middle finger – difficulties in perceiving the fixed and mundane, marriage, money, security, work and stability; under the ring finger – issues with looks, image, creativity, fun and self-expression; beneath the little finger – poor perception in ideas, finance, business, communication or sex.

Any lines (no matter how fine) running from the Air line towards these digits indicate mental interest and connections to these same concerns.

An ideal Air line would be fine and clear with a slight bend, extending to a point between the peacock's feather and antenna finger. This gives a perfect balance between the concrete and the philosophical, the logical and symbolic, and embraces the prevailing worldview without being contained wholly within it. Generally, a clear Air line of good length makes a highly effective character, and a short weak one indicates the reverse.

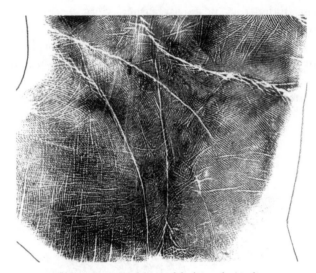

Illustration 97 A good balanced Air line

So-called geniuses tend to have very long Air lines with lots of unusual print markings on palm and digits (usually lots of whorls). Their creative energies are usually powered by large Venus mounts and strong thumbs. As such, they are energetic mavericks, mentally extending the realm of the possible, leaving the prevailing world view behind them with their long, laser-beam minds.

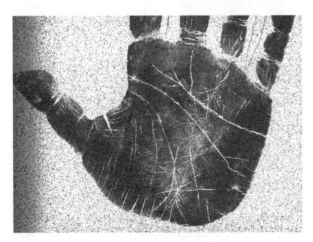

Illustration 98 Einstein's Air line

Remember that whatever the Air line's length, it's more a guide to range and depth of mental perception than how many 'A' levels a person may have. Long lines are drawn towards the refined, specialist and speculative, short to applied mental skills and qualifications. This line's function is always inhibited by poor quality. If it's deep and trench-like, the mind has a tendency to pedantry, dull-mindedness and repetitive patterns of thought.

Bent or straight?

Where the Air line is straight, the mind thinks 'on the level' – direct, logical, objective – the truth is all that matters. The straight line avoids dipping into the sea of emotions represented by the lunar area and dislikes delving into the mysteries of their own psyches. Mental images relate to projections of the exterior world. If they daydream, it tends to feature real people and actual life events, potential or past. Straight lines tend to have a particularly strong and stable mentality, though they can be a little blunt and unsentimental – things are black and white, wrong or right.

Curved Air lines are more subjective, they internalise perceptions and see things more personally. The world takes on different clothes according to the mood they're in and as a reflection of their own experiences. They are more inclined to be artistic and intuitive, their perceptions more coloured, and the journey is more important than the getting there. They'll have more flexibility in the way they see things and defend a point less rigidly than the cold logic of a straight line.

If the Air line is *very* bent, moving deep into the Lunar mount, the person can probe constantly into their inner processes – sometimes being so deep inside themselves that they're unable to connect to others using the common currency of everyday language.

In these cases the light beam is submerged in the inner, watery depths where thinking is not literal but symbolic, where it becomes self referencing and relative to one's own personal mythology, imbued by feelings and dreams. This process is not linear but oblique. On the passive hand, this is a certain sign of a solitary childhood, inner withdrawal and general introversion. Periods of depression and social withdrawal are much more likely with this pattern. The long bent line is common on people who literally or metaphorically lock themselves away and solitarily burrow into dark places: potholers, writers, researchers, archivists, poets, artists and psychoanalysts.

Such people often engage in pedantic or practical work within ordered systems – accountancy, computer programming, advanced maths; not because they have logical minds, but as a way of ordering the world and making sense of it.

A line that continues straight across the hand to touch the outer Mars area on the other side (known as a Sydney line) creates (like all completely crossing lines) a compulsive process. This form of the line shuts off the Lunar quadrant, so the bearer is cut off from their inner feelings; they'll be unsentimental and have a hard edge to their personality.

Such people tend to be strong characters, mentally fixed and physically tense. Though often garrulous and talkative, the urge to be emotionally demonstrative is shut off; they can't relax, though they are great at coping with emotional

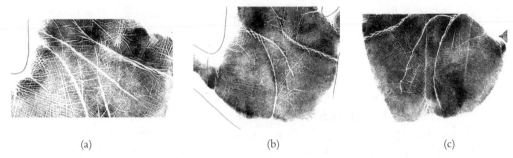

(a)   (b)   (c)

*Illustration 99   A trio of Air lines: (a) straight, (b) bent, (c) curving deep
into the lunar quadrant*

difficulty. They can too easily ignore the demands of the body, instead digesting a
worry or scheme. They'll easily become constipated, sleepless or unable to eat.

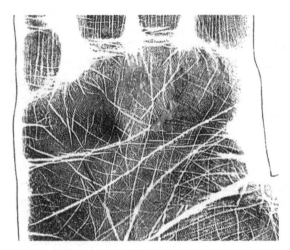

Illustration 100   A Sydney line

The Sydney line on the
passive hand is related to a
tough nurturing experience. It's
also an indicator of a panoramic
mental vision but poor attention
span, dyslexia and potential child
behavioural problems.

On the active hand, though
often highly intelligent, they'll
have had to cope with difficult
life experiences. They may well
be both philosophical yet
obtuse and forgetful. It's as if
the torch beam is locked onto
the far distance, anticipating
events. This is a sort of defence
mechanism – the mind is peren-
nially alert and 'switched on', scanning the darkness to see what lurks ahead.

Beginnings

The beginning of the Air line (where it parts with the Earth line) is highly revealing.
It points out the degree of independence of consciousness.

The greater the gap between the beginning of the line and the Earth line, the
more the person has mentally opened up a gap between themselves and their
roots and the more open-minded they are generally.

If the gap here is very wide on both hands, it's a kind of psychological
separateness, brought on by differing world views within the family. They
would've had to source knowledge outside of the familial environment and

90

think for themselves at an early age; early boarding school attendance is a common cause.

Illustration 101 Large gap between Air and Earth lines

Occasionally, this large gap can simply be a sign of particularly pushy parenting, encouraging boldness, self reliance and personal choice early on. If the beginnings of the Water and Earth lines are clear, this would tend be the case.

People with a large gap here are usually ambitious, apparently confident, upwardly-mobile types. They tend to be bold and adventurous; they 'think big', though to some extent they feel unsupported and have insecurities. It's possible they may 'bite off more than they can chew' in life. They're simply not on the same mental wavelength as their parents, no matter how loving the connection, and there's a sort of rift between themselves and their roots.

Where the line is tied to the Earth line, psychologically one is cautious, one relates to the background, education and formative worldview. One is content to stay within the known mental framework in life and less inclined to move out of one's depth.

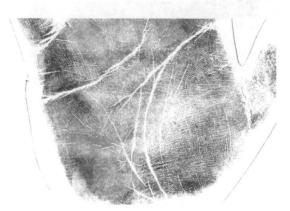

Illustration 102 A 'clinging' Air line

Where the Air line 'clings' to the Earth line excessively, however, it signals psychological dependence and lack of confidence. It's common on members of ultra-orthodox religious groups, particularly where one is brought up within the closed framework of such a group. Such people can't make decisions without reference to the rules and principles, the correct procedure or the canon of accepted belief. Even if the line is long, the source is limited and narrow, and one makes much of a little world.

Where you have the passive Air line tied and the active one with a large gap, you have a person liberated from old limitations, but who manifests them when they visit home.

Commonly, the gap here is much wider on the active hand as one develops independent attitudes, but it may become narrower, indicating greater conservatism.

Often there's a tangle of lines here. This shows complex patterns of insecurity and confidence within specific areas – the sort of person who bursts with lofty confidence in the work team but is inhibited with family, for instance.

Occasionally, the beginning part of the Air line is missing. This would show no early memory and late mental development.

More rarely, the line leaps upward from the Earth line at an angle with sudden rebellion and the abrupt awakening of individualism.

If the line's beginning has a line linking it to the Mars mount, the person will have called on great courage in life and there'll be a pushy aspect to the character. If this Mars connection is the *only* beginning, they'll be particularly bullish and may see conflict in the most innocuous situation.

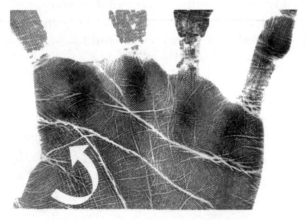

Illustration 103 Link line to Mars mount

Forks, breaks, branches and doubled lines

Forks at the *end* of the Air line introduce diversity to the character; a small branch here is often called a 'writer's fork'. Writers often have this sign, but mental agility and an ability to make practical expression of inspiration is the meaning. Where the fork is large, the personality has mental diversity that loves, for example, the introspective poetry of Sylvia Plath, as well as embracing the perspective of a level-headed pragmatist.

It's important to note that the Air line is one of the quickest to change; a person with a chaotic line needs to be advised to develop concentration. A still point held in the mind through persistence in one task at a time will bear results. A short line will often lengthen when a broad, holistic subject is studied, e.g. comparative philosophy.

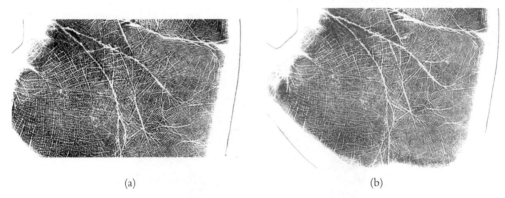

(a)   (b)

Illustration 104 (a) Before and (b) after a literature degree

Where the line breaks and renews itself, it illustrates a massive change in personality where one sees the world very differently – often even the speech patterns change. The person may well look back on the past as if it happened to someone else.

Always keep hand shape, skin texture and antenna finger in mind; these define the context of the Air line.

In the rare case of the Air line being doubled, there's a psychological duality and doubling of the personality.

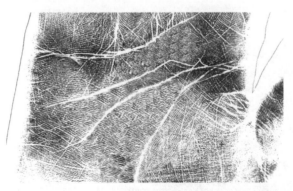

Illustration 105 Doubled Air line. This woman is bilingual and is a markedly different person in each language

Two Air lines create someone who has two very different mental frameworks and two different personalities in which to operate. They will think and function differently in the two different contexts. For instance, someone may have different personalities completely within the realms of business and family. If the two lines are well separated these aspects of life will be kept well apart in the person's life.

Short lines parallel to and floating above the Air line are parts of consciousness that 'float' above normal awareness. These aren't always accessible. The floating lines are part of a more elevated vision available in certain circumstances and in a particular milieu. This can mean, for instance, that only when we're with our development group or a particularly stimulating friend are we able to perceive angels or display a surreal wit.

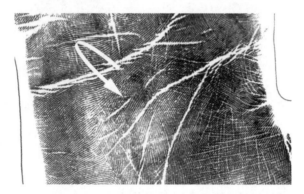

Illustration 106 Floating lines above the Air line

Lots of lines running off the main line towards the fingers indicate too many influences, someone who has loads of issues and who listens to many different people, getting muddled trying to agree with all of them.

A bar line on the percussion above the end of the Air line is like a mini Sydney line – it's a response to a tough, unpampered background and indicates a long period of striving. It's related to a negative nurturing experience by the mother figure and it's a sure sign of an ambitious personality who's never satisfied, as if the person is continually striving to reach up to the mark.

Sometimes (in around 1% of people), the Air line and Water line are joined completely into a single line, known as a simian line.

Illustration 107 A bar line above the end of the Air line

This is the sign of an intense, obsessive personality. One of the lines is subverted to the other – usually it's the feelings of the Water line subverted into the Air line, but it can be the reverse. Water dominated simian lines are higher up the palm than Air dominant ones.

Simian-lined folk are like a repressed, silently raging storm; thought and feeling are synonymous. They put all their feelings and ideas into their goals in a relentless,

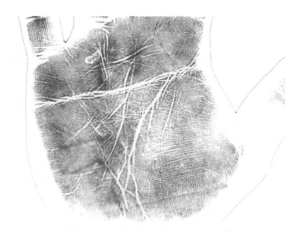

Illustration 108 A simian line

single-minded manner. This, of course, can lead to great achievements and indeed it's disproportionately found on highly successful people, particularly in fields where absolute dedication is necessary: professional athletes, intellectuals, meticulous researchers, self-made business magnates.

As the Water and Air lines are running together, they tend to be emotionally and psychologically closed people, socially awkward, solitary, highly repressed with one-track minds. They're unable to be frivolous or jump from one subject to another. They find it difficult to relax and are often unconcerned about their appearance.

Simian-line folk tend to get stuck in patterns – never letting go of their novel idea, business plan, grudge against an employer, family commitments or ex-partner. Once in a relationship they rarely let go of it. There is always extremism of thought, feeling or deed present.

A simian line can give an otherwise unremarkable hand great potential, through sheer relentlessness.

Religious fanatics and criminals also have disproportionately high numbers of simian lines, and their intense focus can blind them to the feelings of others. It occurs to a hugely disproportionate degree in Down's Syndrome (55%), but the line here is

Illustration 109 Tony Blair's simian line

Water line dominance over the Air line's thought process. Where you see a simian line, always check for the presence of a good Fire line (soon to be studied) and a good thumb. Such intensity needs to be well managed. Advise creative relaxation to all with a simian line.

EXERCISE

Look at your own Earth and Air lines. How do you experience the qualities found there? Compare your passive and active lines. Look at the prints of five people you know. Ask them about their family and background, their feelings of permanence and their sense of security. Compare the Air lines in a similar way, ask if they're philosophical or practical, test their openness to ideas, how they see the future. See if you can see a relationship between these people's lines and the way they experience life. Put your observations in your journal.

8

The Water and Fire Lines

We'll consider the remaining two major lines now, which are generally more variable in form than the two previous ones. Each line reflects a different aspect of a person and its inevitable you'll come across line patterns you've never seen before. By understanding the line's general principle you can interpret any major line with ease. The Water and Fire are about our interaction with, and assimilation of, exterior forces.

Water (heart) line

The Water line is like a river of receptivity that allows feeling, intuition, emotional response and ideals to flow within us. Its course runs from the percussion edge under the little finger in the Mercury-ruled communication quadrant, to the personal quadrant of the hand. Thus it connects the sense of self with the outside world. Always read this line in conjunction with the skin quality, the gauge of receptive sensitivity.

Sadly, in the modern Western world it's common to see Water lines somewhat broken and corrupted, which must be a reflection of our decayed emotional culture. Probably the closing up of this stream is a necessary concession to modern conditions: living densely packed together in a materialistic society, the blurring of sexual roles, parental break-ups and the general lack of harmony in our surroundings.

The depth of the line reflects the depth of feeling; a deep, red line reflects deep and powerful passions, where a faint, shallow line is more reticent.

A straight line is direct and somewhat unsubtle. The river of feeling rushes towards the goal of affections with little ado or preamble; a curved line is more graceful and romantic.

If the Water line is broken, there's a break in the continuity of relationships and a hesitation in the expression of feelings and the response to emotive stimuli. A dancer with this characteristic won't be able to give himself completely to the music; there'll be a schism in his responses.

Breaks are symptomatic of a break of relationship chronologically (though timing is very difficult to judge on this line) restricting the ability to feel. When the line restarts there's an emotional renewal into new emotional experiences. Try to see this line as not simply the pattern of the person's love life, but their overall emotional flow, their empathy with others, their spiritual ideals and their sense of connectedness. This line is about the ability to respond to a painting, a caress or a scent. Without this line we'd be coldly mechanical and logical, like robots.

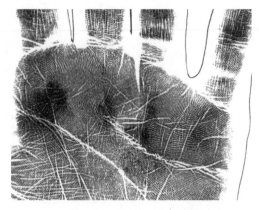

Illustration 110 A poor quality Water line

If the line is a chain of islands, the bearer will be moody, changeable and often lost in the turbulence of their emotions.

Lines branching off the main line going up to the fingers reflect higher, more idealistic yearnings and experiences and dropping lines are inclined to fearfulness and insecurity.

An ideal Water line would be clear, curve like a crescent moon and end between the index and middle digits. This is rare, however.

A good Water line is no guarantee of a perfect love life, but the bearer would have a natural sense of beauty, aesthetics and sexuality; they'd be optimistic, without being unrealistic; romantic, poetic and spiritual without deserting the sensual; their parents would have demonstrated strongly defined sexual roles. This is a balance of ideals and practicality, responsiveness, compassion and naturalism. Bearers of such lines are optimistic romantics and can't ever be truly cynical.

It's normal for this line to be somewhat jagged at the beginning on modern, Western-born people, as the emotions initially adjust to the constraints of the exterior world.

Occasionally, the Water line is low set, starting close to the Air line, further down than normal. This denotes emotions that are deep under the surface. There's always tremendous emotional caution and reticence in such cases, also emotional pragmatism but loyalty in abundance once initial reserve is won over.

When reading the Water line, the second half of the line (from beneath

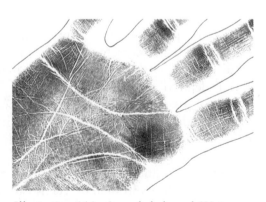

Illustration 111 A good, balanced Water line

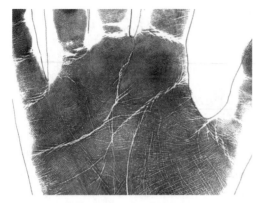

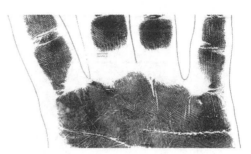

Illustration 112 A low set Water line   *Illustration 113 A short Water line*

the centre of the palm towards the index finger) varies hugely; this section is absolutely paramount.

If the line is short and straight, ending under or before the middle finger, the emotions don't connect to the personal area of the palm and, therefore, the person can't connect to others – they lack empathy. They'll be blunt, unresponsive and maybe even unfeeling towards others. If found with coarse skin, it can be the sign of a sociopath who shuns the company of others. It's as if they're locked inside with no way to express or know their feelings.

The opposite pattern, where the line crosses the palm completely from side to side, creates an obsessive pattern where they can't stop responding to others. Though extremely compassionate and caring souls, they simply *can't* say no. Very long lines are extremely common on all sorts of therapists and carers. As the line is flat, not curving to a more abstract ideal, they demonstrate emotions practically. Curiously, such people often have unfulfilling personal love lives. If there's no upward branch to the line, a torrent of emotion floods across the hand, blocking the demonstrative process and rendering them repressive and unlikely to whisper the words of love, yet they're full of caring devotion. Often the demands of others put great strains on personal relationships.

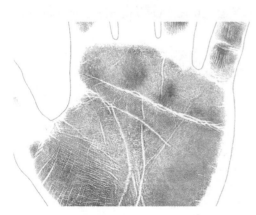

Illustration 114 A very long Water line

Long straight lines a little shorter than this, ending under the index finger, are loving and passionate, but are lacking idealism. It's as if the goal of their emotions is paramount; but they can be uncertain exactly who their ideal love mate truly is once the chase is over. Such love as this must never be

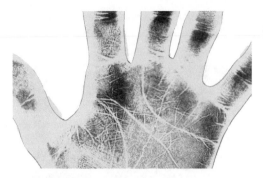

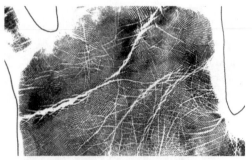

Illustration 115 Water line curving into the wall digit

Illustration 116 Water line that breaks and drops to the Earth line. This person suffered a traumatic divorce

taken for granted lest they pursue other conquests. Straight, red lines are passionate and usually highly sexual.

If the line curves up into the middle (wall) finger, there's an emotional idealism, but it's restricted to the permanent connections in one's life, i.e. long-term partner, family, long-standing friends; such people tend to keep lots of pets. These aren't romantically adventurous folk – they express love by the giving and receiving of presents. Often deeply loyal and loving people, they can be overly concerned with the house and family and wearing the 'right' dress at the wedding. Social obligations weigh heavily upon them.

Such people would definitely go for solid Steve rather than wild Warren, plain Jane over comely Bethany. They'll choose security rather than passion. Enormous sacrifices are made to provide material security for the children and, indeed, any traditional emotional duty such as obligation to parents.

When the Water line fractures, with a falling line reaching towards the Earth line, it signifies the negative expectation of or actual experience of severe loss.

A Water line reaching up to the base of the index finger creates emotional idealism pitched rather high, because the digit of self reflects a particularly personal ideal.

If the line is also deep and red, this could show a particularly optimistic person with a great sense of romanticism. Often it's a sign of a need for a spiritual aspect to life. However, it's often found on people who put their partners on a pedestal. Though they often have an admirable sense of seeing the best in people; it's hard for them to be satisfied with the mundane – they pine for the greener grass of a more beautiful love or a more divine aspect to life. It can create a wistful restlessness and it's crucial that this is pointed out to the bearer.

An extremely common ending is for a section of the water line to be broken off.

This is where the ending of the line has drifted away and floats higher up the palm. The higher part is an aspect akin to an emotional 'shop window'. This means they partially respond to others superficially, but without engaging the

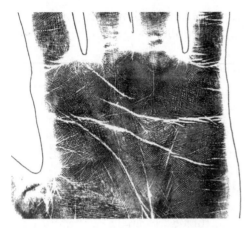

Illustration 117 A broken-off Water line

real feelings as represented by the main part of the line.

Though apparently open enough, someone with a broken-off line is actually hard to know and sometimes an enigma to themselves emotively.

This disconnection of feeling isn't a cynical ploy but a response to the complexity of social situations, where we've learned to feel one thing and appear to feel another. It's a somewhat modern development. This is particularly prevalent among the young, where a mood of post-modern irony is the prevailing norm. This entails affecting a style or an emotional front, making it difficult to be open-hearted and spontaneously effusive. The early experience of divorce and emotional disappointment is, of course, common to so many of us and so is this line. Such a pattern means chronologically, a much happier second marriage or emotive attainment in later life, when a different level of sentiment (the broken off part) is attained.

This kind of broken-off, extra section to the Water lines are ideal for those who deal with the public and need a professional 'front'.

The greater the gap between the two segments, the greater the schism between social face and inner drive. When the gap is truly huge, one often needs to be with others constantly, to maintain the buoyancy of mood lest one drops into the sink of the deeper, more restrained and more intensely private hurts of the lower line.

A dropping single ending to the Water line often signifies same-sex orientation – but our sexuality is more fluid than we'd like to admit so be extremely judicious with this interpretation.

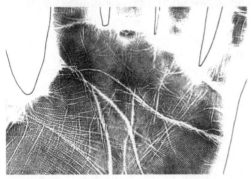

Illustration 118 Dropping ending to the Water line

Where the line drops all the way down to touch the Earth line or comes close to it there's a sense of needing to hold onto someone to stabilise and root oneself. It's a clear sign of emotional insecurity and traditionally it signals some experience of personal tragedy; certainly there'll be fear of loss and also tremendous jealousy.

A branch from the Water line touching the Earth line usually indicates a very strong connection to parents.

Indeed, someone who *can't let go* of their parents and family; though it can indicate the reverse and a desperate desire for this kind of support. It's seen where parents weren't demonstrative emotionally.

This signals the person needs lots of emotional support and proof of commitment. They're likely to be sentimental, dwelling on the past and hoarding love mementoes. It's difficult for them to let go in relationships – they can hold on far too long in hopeless cases.

If this is the only or dominant ending to the Water line, they may well settle for a partner who could be considered a somewhat easy victory on love's battlefield; someone who's perhaps less than their match.

If a falling line drops all the way to the Mars mount this is often an indication of loss of a close relationship and subsequent depression. It's been linked to diabetes and the death of a partner, which is itself a trigger in the development of this disease.

Multiple endings

In a cunning ploy to thwart us palmists, the Water line often has forked or multiple endings. In such cases you must understand this to indicate multiple levels of emotion.

You may encounter a Water line which drops to the Earth line for instance, with a second floating section above it. This indicates a cool, upbeat exterior and an underlying experience or fear of loss, which makes for a dread of dependency. It's easy to be physically, but not emotionally, close to such people. Only where they can open up to their underlying anxieties does true intimacy take place.

It's hard to admit to jealous and dependent urges and such people can be in somewhat deep denial. They often cannot let go of old relationships, aware that somehow a chance was missed.

Alternatively there may be both a romantic, idealistic curved line and also a dropping, insecure line seeking the 'safe rock' of the Earth line. One line may run straight across the hand, ceaselessly giving to others, and this may be combined with a branch that romantically reaches up between the index and middle fingers; there are endless possibilities.

Wherever there are multiple endings, simply interpret all the qualities of each ending, emphasising the strongest one (if one is indeed stronger).

Multiple endings explain the contra-dictions, confusions and uncertainties we bring to relationships; explaining these can be enormously powerful and cathartic to the bearer.

Illustration 119 A Water line with multiple endings

Lots of little lines shooting out of the end of the Water line signals a natural flirt, with lots of connections to different types of people.

Mini simian lines

Where little lines connect the Air and Water lines together, these are like 'short circuits' that create fixed and obsessive emotive patterns. They're a form of mini simian line. Always they're found under the middle or ring fingers.

Under the middle finger there's an obsession with family, security and fixed relationships. No matter how zany in other ways, they'll work hard for such aims. Such people can't let go of commitments and need to be firmly married

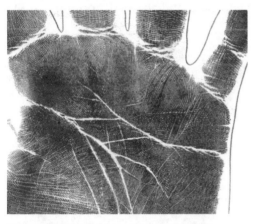

Illustration 120 Lines joining Air and Water lines

or not at all. Ironically, they often experience loss or threat to what they hold onto, though this mark gives a stoicism to help repair the loss.

A line connecting to the Air line under the ring finger indicates an obsession with being popular and winning over the opposite sex, often creativity is ignored for social success.

Islands on the Water line are emotionally confusing periods which are hard to time accurately. Timing on this line begins at the little finger end, with the age of forty being under the join of the middle and ring digits; but time measurement is crude on this line.

A poor Water line can be quickly improved by learning to trust one's feelings and developing non-logical awareness through, for instance, meditation, dance or singing.

Fire line (fate, Saturn) line

This is the most variable of the main lines and is more often than not only partially present. Its individuality makes it very revealing in interpretation. It's quite common for this line not to develop at all until well after adolescence.

The line may begin low down in the centre of the palm, or start somewhere in the lunar quadrant or rise up from the Earth line. It may have the lower or other sections missing, be broken into fragments, or be doubled. Occasionally it's missing altogether, and only very rarely is it found in its complete form from palm base to the bottom of the middle digit. Note that only lines or sections of lines pointing to the middle 'wall' finger are true Fire lines.

Imagine this line as a 'firewall'. Both in computer terminology and around medieval castles, a firewall is a barrier against intrusion. In the hand it forms a burning pathway delineating character, establishing our personal path in life, defining goals, lifestyle, habits, personal values and loyalties from all the possibilities and distractions society bombards us with.

It moves towards the structured, boundary-creating realm of the 'wall digit' and as such, establishes personal aims where we can focus and apply ourselves, particularly in terms of career choice.

Only where the complete line is found from base to finger, does this line take on the old-fashioned meaning of the 'fate' line. This exceptional length gives a fixed, fated attitude, as if the firewalls are too high and the path too long to see any possibility of personal alternative to one's life path.

Bearers of this long line have little sense of choice. They doggedly pursue their life-course burdened with a world-weary sense of being destined to their path, feeling life offers no alternative. This may have its benefits – mastery of one's profession or goal may come through such doggedness; the yogi may reach guru status through never missing a day of her devotions over a whole lifetime. However, if this sign is on the hand of a car-park attendant it may not bode so well. All bearers of this sign need to be counselled into seeing that they have choice. They must see that they can switch

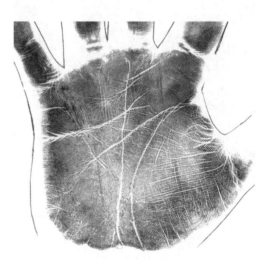

Illustration 121 A Fire line in its complete form

career, take time off and try diverse experiences: anything from Morris dancing to breeding stoats; subsequently, the line will grow branches and relax its borders.

Where there's no Fire line at all, there's a sense of not having found oneself – one has no sense of what one is defined by, no *individual* character and no idea of what work and lifestyle one wants.

Without the presence of a Fire line a person is somewhat rudderless. A good *Earth* line can compensate by giving good roots that binds one to familial, traditional or peer patterns. One simply follows the manual of convention. Typically this means a job in a large structure or institution, sustaining the character until a Fire line develops. Often this will be found beginning half way up the palm, coinciding with the age of thirty or so.

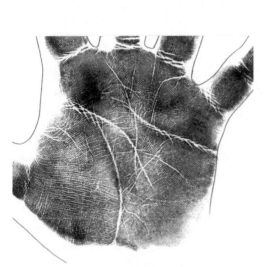

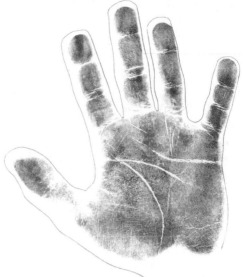

Illustration 122 A typical partial Fire line   *Illustration 123 Earth hand with no Fire line*

On a solid, square-palmed, short-fingered Earth hand with a naturally fixed, traditional nature, the Fire line may never develop. They cheerfully plough the path their parents, tradition or necessity dictates. This could mean simply devoting themselves to parenting on a woman's hand, otherwise they'll follow the well-trodden path of family profession or an institutional career – such hands are never self-employed.

Whenever the Fire line is missing and the Earth line is strong, there's a drive to define oneself within a structure, with a formulaic application. Local government work, university or the military are good examples, anywhere there's a pre-estab-lished pattern and code for life goals with no real individualistic or personal input.

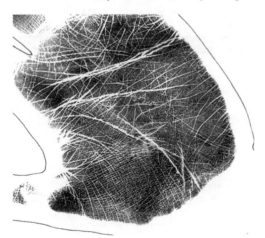

Where there's no Fire line on a more complex, long-fingered, fine-skinned, or multi-lined hand and no clear Earth line, this is a much more difficult situation.

Such people are adrift in life with no boundaries and no clear goals. A strong thumb will establish stability eventually, but if there are undermining qualities, like a composite pattern on the thumb, or radial loop on the index finger, they are often unbalanced and

Illustration 124 Full hand with no Fire line

unstable. They simply don't know what they want or who they are. They need to establish clear, appropriate goals and stick to them, no matter what, and the Fire line will manifest itself. When this line appears, one's life attains purpose, structure, stability and balance.

Complex hands with no Fire lines often linger in university until their thirties, then commit themselves to the wrong people, do the wrong jobs and follow all sorts of bandwagons, only gaining a sense of direction when the Fire line manifests itself.

The lack of a Fire line means there's little in the way of personal ethics and beliefs. It's an irony that many people in the public eye – and many a devout follower of fashion, cause, cult or coven – are actually followers because they lack a Fire line and an individual life path; ah maya, all is maya.

The lack of a Fire line is at the heart of much behaviour that's immature and incoherent, as we struggle with the longing to come home to ourselves. The presence of one's own firewall gives a sense of balance and acceptance and of taking up the burden of willing responsibility.

Unfortunately, the lack of this line is becoming endemic and it's certainly deteriorated in the past twenty years while I've been reading hands. Thankfully it can develop quickly.

Modern society is itself becoming more 'fiery' – so full of easy ways to define ourselves through, for instance, clothes, politics, car or musical allegiances that we're less able to blaze our own pathway. Our culture is so powerful in its pressures that it overwhelms our personal fences.

Always advise people without this line to define themselves by keeping a personal journal, one that records with absolute honesty, not events, but their own insights, reflections and feelings; in such manner is self definition realised.

Note that when this line is weak or missing, it's not a sign of lack of success – only that one can't be successful *in one's own terms*. The merchant banker will often display a very weak version of this line, so *worldly* success is not the issue. The school cleaner with this line would be much more likely to be fulfilled, because she's following her own path in her own way. The strength of the line is how well entrenched you are in your own values, how protected you are from the common, corporate or received ideals.

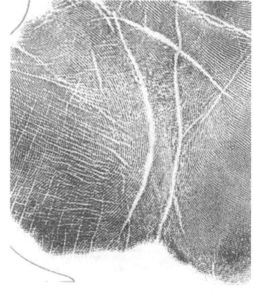

Illustration 125 A good clear Fire line

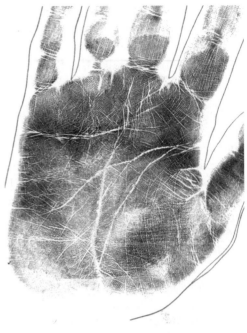

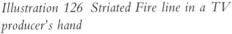

Illustration 126 Striated Fire line in a TV producer's hand

Illustration 127 An overemphatic Fire line

If the Fire line is striated, it's as if the person's defining firewall is breaking down and outside influences pervade the soul. There's a striving, stressful attitude to work and achievement.

This is found on careerists whose job lends status and prestige. However, it's about getting an identity through work, rather than about getting personal satisfaction within it. It's common in those sexy, high profile vocations – the media, law, advertising etc. Striated lines are much more liable to breakdown and to wander off their paths in life, because without the trappings of success they're weakly defined people.

The opposite characteristic, where the Fire line's *extremely* bold, so that it's stronger than any other line, is also problematic.

If the Fire line is the strongest line, they're liable to be difficult, uncompromising people and very strong characters. They define the world in their own terms. Everyone can seem to be against them; they're fighting to be themselves and gain their goals against perceived pressure from all fronts – stuck behind their blazing walls. Often people with strong Fire lines dominate their environments, profession or circumstances.

Beginnings

The position from which the line grows is crucial. If it starts in the centre of the hand, near the palm base, this is a good position, indicating early responsibility and a balanced personality. Often such people become precociously mature with common sense beyond their early years.

If the line originates in the lunar quadrant of the hand, there's an emphasis on using the emotions and the personal, feminine side. It's much more likely that work will revolve around their ability to get along with others, and that relationships are prioritised in their lives.

This is very common on those who work in small groups and in creative, media or any people based profession: customer relations, hairdressing, personnel management, beauty therapy.

Their life balance comes from people, so they're naturally good at schmoozing, socialising and responding to others. This is the path of adaptability and indicates drawing on one's deeper inner (lunar) drives and moving away from parental preferences as a basis for life goals. The person develops emotive, rather than corporate or familial ambitions.

Where a line *joins* an existing Fire line from the lunar quadrant, or a new Fire line from the lunar quadrant replaces a previous one, it indicates a time in mid–life where one wants more from work: more satisfaction, time off, personal input, variety, influence. It can indicate a new commitment or relationship that alters one's goals – new friendships or a fascination with alternative values, for instance, are often indicated like this.

Where the line *curves* deeply from within the lunar quadrant, there'll be an unusual job and lifestyle and an aversion to conventional life patterns. Such people usually have strong reticence about commitment to anything. This line makes for an eccentric, off centre, unpredictable individual who has consciously avoided their background and to some extent is isolated and self-protective.

Straight lines are consistent in aims and direction; bent ones change character, direction and goals as time progresses.

Where the Fire line originates from the Earth line, they will base their goals on their 'root', their background and education and be much less individual and more conventional. It's as if they've internalised a set of values from their formative influences and feel bound to them. Status is conferred upon them from an exterior source and they march on the road placed before them in life.

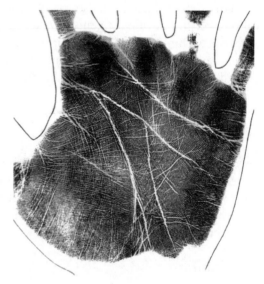

Illustration 128 Fire line from lunar quadrant

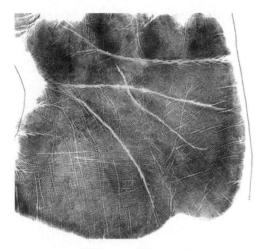

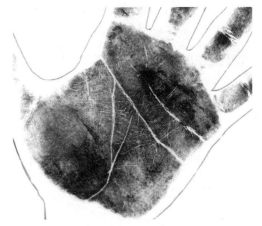

Illustration 130 Fire line emerging from within the Earth line, with similarly 'bound' Air and Earth lines (this person works in the family business and still hasn't left home at 38)

Illustration 129 Bent Fire line from lunar quadrant

A Fire line emerging from *within* the Earth line is found on people with the same profession as their parents. It's as if they're planted well into the soil of their formative influences. This pattern is far more bound to received codes than not having a Fire line at all.

If this sign if accompanied by an Air line which is similarly 'bound' to the Earth line on the passive hand, it's certain that family and background has stifled independent thought. It's found on the offspring of strict religious groups, or in any situation where one's not invited to question authority.

At the point in chronological time where the line shoots from the Earth line (usually late in life, 50 years and up) they may well develop their own life path and free themselves from defining influences.

It's normal for the Fire line to expire around the junction to the Air or Water lines. Often there are a series of little Fire lines up above the Water line, these signal roles we establish in old age – part-time work, hobbies or duty to grand-children.

Islands in the Fire line indicate periods of unemployment, often bankruptcy or lack of any kind of fulfilment. Sometimes they indicate a complete loss of identity within a large organisation or relationship.

EXERCISE

Look at your own hands and those of ten people you know, and compare their Water and Fire lines with yours. You'll probably be surprised at the very different nature of the emotional processes and goal orientations that you see. Ask people about their experiences of emotions and sense of personal goals.

Give someone you don't know a written reading, going over all you've studied so far. Do this in writing from an annotated print without them being present to make you nervous. Use this book as a reference. Write their reactions to the reading in your journal.

9

No Minor Matter – the Minor and Subsidiary Lines

The minor lines are often completely missing, half-formed and are hugely individualistic in their manifestation. As with the major lines, the underlying principles are hugely important. Minor lines tend to be very changeable. They're seams of gold to be mined, full of rich potentials and characteristics.

As a general rule, where a minor line *is* present, if it's clear and of good quality, it's a beneficial sign giving an extra facility to the person. Where a minor line is striated, broken-up, islanded or otherwise poor in quality, its indications are generally negative.

When you find the rare case of a minor line being the *strongest* of all the lines, there's a problem: the person's life force is fixated in a way that undermines their ability to function normally. It's an indication of psychological or physical imbalance.

We'll go through the minor lines from the top of the palm, and work downward, then we'll cover the subsidiary markings.

Mirage line (Ring of Saturn, Neptune line, Girdle of Venus)

This line floats above the Water line, and is often fragmentary in form. It's easy to confuse it with a broken-off section of the Water line.

Imagine this as a secondary, higher Water line, which gives an emotional response to purely abstract experience.

In traditional palmistry it's associated with Saturn and an exaggerated sensuality, but it's meaning is much closer to that of the planet Neptune, which rules illusions and visions.

When present in clear form, it gives a vivid imagination and an ineffable drive to escape the mundane to higher worlds. This creates a need for time and space to dream and stimulates responsiveness to myth, symbols and visions. This may manifest as a lover of art galleries, a classic film buff, a scriptwriter, a spiritual seeker, a 'Trekkie', an inspired artist or master of cyberspace.

Negatively, it's associated with drug taking, and with cosmic types – 'on another planet', fatuous thinkers and introverts; those who prefer dreams to reality.

Like any line, much depends on other qualities – particularly the quality of the Air and Earth lines. It's always a potential gift to the imagination and creative possibilities.

If the rational aspect is good, indicated by a clear balanced Air line and the person is well-grounded, indicated by a half-decent Earth line, the bearer may reach for the stars and bring to Earth in practical form the music and inspiration of the heavenly spheres.

It's common on composers who 'hear' the music as they write; writers who live their characters; craftsmen who 'see' the finished work.

If the Air line is weak and the Earth line poor or missing its bottom section, there can be a distinctly wobbly mindset, one that construes conspiracy theory, karmic consequence or high drama from the most ordinary experience. This line often creates an

Illustration 131 A well-marked mirage line

irrational visionary, perfectionist or hedonist constantly seeking to escape to a richer level of experience.

Wherever it's found clearly presented, it adds a quality of sympathy, general sensitivity and a wistful romanticism – also a love of luxury and of the finer things in life.

On the rare example on a coarse-skinned hand, with large base finger phalanges, there may well be the old-fashioned meaning of a drive to escape into sensual excess.

On either gender, where this line is found there's a marked tendency to seek out strong partners, more level-headed and responsible than themselves.

It's problematic when this line is as strong as, or stronger than, the Water line. Then there's a double layer of feeling experience, the bearer can't connect intimately in a direct emotional manner. This can be the preserve of the moody, complex, fantasist.

Wherever the mirage line's strong, there's a refusal to be 'realistic'. Such people will never let go of their illusions and indeed, to them, visions are a part of life.

The difficulty can be that, though they see themselves as great romantics, they can actually love more the memory, the ideal, or the projected experience than the reality. They suffer the irony of seeing themselves beset by romantic yearning, but rarely live such impulses out – real life isn't perfect enough. Only when actuality has been rendered into myth or maybe do they internalise emotions, this is the stuff of poets, dreamers and spiritual wanderers.

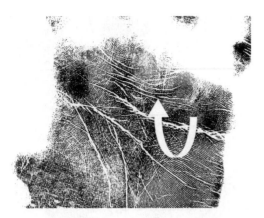

Illustration 132 A fragmented Mirage line

It's difficult also, on the rare occasions when the line plunges into the Water line, because at some point in their lives there's a clash between ideals and reality: their adored guru makes a pass at them, the white knight abandons his maiden, their allotted star falls from heaven.

Always compare this line to the Air and Water lines to see how the emotive ideals compare with the actual levels of emotional and rational experience.

In fragmented form, this line produces an extremely sensitive and introverted emotive state. This gives a highly-strung nature; though receptive to others, there's often an attraction to hallucinogenic experiences. Such people are more easily disorientated than most.

Affection lines

On the extreme outer edge of the palm, beneath the little finger and above the Water line, are the attachment lines (you may have to turn the palm edge-on to see these lines).

Traditionally, all sorts of nonsense has been perpetrated about these lines, linking them with marriages and, in particular, the number and gender of children.

Basically, ignore these lines completely unless they extend well into the palm and manifest as an island, a long straight line, a line which curves sharply up around the Air finger's base, or one that falls down to the Water line. In any of these (moderately rare) cases, the line becomes very significant indeed. Any noteworthy line here, in the sexual and communicative area of the palm, is a hidden template for emotional ideals.

A typical affection line barely projects into the surface of the palm at all. If a line reaches two centimetres or more into the palm, a tremendous search for the 'right' partner will dominate the person's love life. They're always on the lookout for their soul-mate. Early relationships can be seriously undermined by this trait, but once their ideal is eventually found they tend to be totally devoted and rarely suffer a parting from the object of their affections.

Where an affection line plunges towards the Water line or actually crosses it, there's a negative experience or impulse, a subliminal inclination to a difficult relationship.

Where seen, there's a very high incidence of divorce or serious losses in love. Bearers seem to set themselves up for such encounters; these lines need to be explained and understood so suffering can be averted.

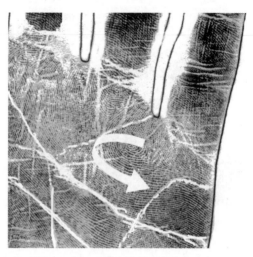

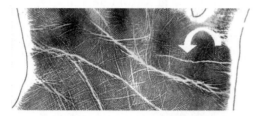

Illustration 133 An extended affection line

Illustration 134 A plunging affection line –
this is a three time divorcée

Where the line cuts upward around the little finger, it seems to cut off the sexual and communicative facility of this digit. Such people stay outside of the mating game for long periods; they may endure long, celibate relationships. It's as if the sexual facility is 'ring fenced' by this line and there could well be some sexual hang-ups.

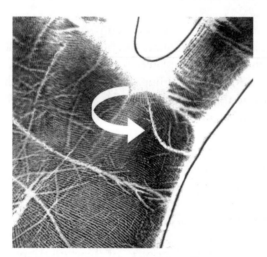

Illustration 135 An encircling affection line

Where there's an affection line ending in an island, there's a distorted, unclear view of relationships. It's an indication of having no clear ideal and of someone who finds it difficult to plight their troth wholeheartedly. They'll be tentative with the object of their affections, and get into messy 'holding' relationship situations.

Thankfully, whenever any negative manifestation of this line is fully brought to light, it tends to lose its hold on the bearer.

Passion line

This one always gets everyone's attention! I've conducted research into over a thousand adherents to pornography, partner swapping and other sexual predilections and discovered this line endemic to such folk. The passion line is a straight, angular line running from somewhere around the mid-section of the Water line and moving up towards the base of the little finger.

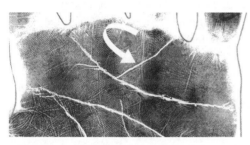

Illustration 136 The passion line

It's an indication of a highly visual and responsive sexuality, someone who definitely prefers to keep the lights on! Where you have a clear and complete example of this line, you have someone that takes sex very seriously and who needs colour, variety and passion in their sex lives.

It's found particularly on those who enjoy voyeuristic sexual experiences and those who respond to the visual and imaginative side of sex.

I've found many examples of this among authors of 'black lace' type risqué novels, and among those in the sex industry and on internet porn addicts it's always present. The bearers can be mesmerised by sexual ideals and can easily confuse sexual infatuation with love.

The line is often found in fragmentary form, which denotes a restless sexual imagination but in a more fragmented and wistful manner. Such people are always curious about other people's sex lives and don't necessarily live out their own fantasies.

Note that this line represents a heightened abstract and visual aspect to sexuality and doesn't necessarily mean the person has a high *drive*. This is more the preserve of the state of

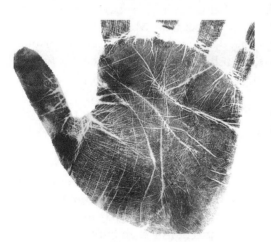

*Illustration 137 of Cynthia Payne's palm
(the notorious brothel madam)*

health, and of the Venus mount and the Water line itself. Though the presence of this sign normally lends a general lustiness, the sexual drive is universal and lacking the line won't compromise anyone's sexuality.

The passion line is like a quiet reel of erotic possibilities running on the back of the mind, literally someone that has 'sex on the brain'. Be very careful when pointing this out as it can cause great embarrassment and is always guaranteed to get people worked up – either because they have one, or because they don't!

When this line actually *crosses* the Water line and runs downwards,

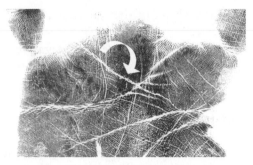

Illustration 138 Note the passion line here is as strong as (if not stronger than) the Water line which it crosses. This person will connect to the opposite sex primarily in sexual terms – it's a pornographic film maker's hand

towards the Earth line, you have someone who is inclined to be sexually jealous and possessive. They'll want the upper hand sexually, and may be inclined to be sexually manipulative.

Apollo line (line of sun)

This is another of many examples where the time-honoured interpretation needs to updated in the light of modern developments.

This line is invariably very fine and is situated under the ring finger. Its customary meaning is that it's a sign of fame and public acclaim, but in these days of instant and easy celebrity by people with no talent, this is no longer true. Most famous people in the modern sense are unlikely to sport this line, displaying instead a lack of personal goals and a desperate need for attention (shown by an over-long peacock's feather digit and a missing Fire line). The palm in Illustration 49 is a good example; note the lack of any noteworthy Apollo line.

This line is nearly always present above the Water line and under the ring finger and is of no consequence here. It's when it begins further down, from around the level of the Air line or lower, that it is significant.

Its presence signals a sense of oneness with a process, a need for peace and quiet, a sense of contentment and an inner life. The bearers have an ability to disconnect or 'tune out' the outer world. Usually this is by complete absorption in some meditative or artistic activity. It's found on spiritual healers, meditators, therapists, artists and anyone completely immersed in the process of their work or hobby. This can also include those utterly absorbed and content simply weeding the garden.

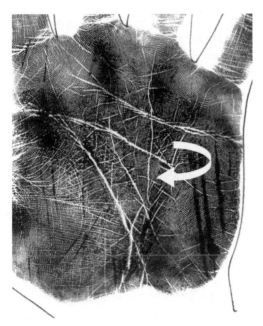

Illustration 139 A complete Apollo line

People with this line need peace and time alone so that they can forget the outer world. It shows a connection to a higher, ego-less inner sanctum.

Introspective types – writers, artists and others who have some connection to an inner realm through their work – tend to develop these lines, but also anyone who finds solitary peace and inner tranquillity in any activity.

Far from being a sign of fame, it signals someone who's perfectly content in their inner world who will shun the limelight. When this appears on the hand, worldly demands are usually sacrificed to watch the sunset or potter in the studio.

This line in its longer form is much more likely on the reclusive, J. D. Salinger type artist than on any film star. Sadly, the rarity of this line on the hands of the famous shows how superficial most 'stars' actually are.

We've replaced the development of an inner peace with the cult of stardom; celebrities tend to perpetuate themselves by remaining in the limelight and never retreating inside. It's actually far more common on the contented embroiderer or angler.

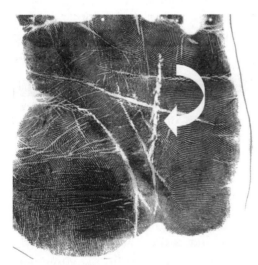

Illustration 140 An overdeveloped Apollo line

If present only on the active hand, the line is most likely connected with work and would indicate that they work alone. If only on the passive hand, it relates to hobbies or home activity.

As previously noted, most people have a section of an Apollo line above the Water line. This marks a period in latter life when we retire and find a kind of gentle peace. You could see the presence of this sign as an indicator of contentment.

Beware this line when it's very strong. If stronger than the main lines (remember, no minor line should be stronger than a major one), it's likely to be someone extremely introverted, someone who may 'hear voices' or who can't do anything without 'consulting spirit'. At the least it shows an exceptionally introverted and unworldly person who can't bear reality without tuning out of it constantly.

Mercury (hepatica) line

This is best visualised as an adjunct to the Air line. It's like an extra, lateral aspect to mental activity that's connected physically with the autonomic nervous system.

When (as it often is) missing, there can be a lack of awareness of bodily processes: someone unaware of fatigue, indigestion or the subtler levels of their physical body.

If this line is fine and clear, it acts as a stimulus to the Air line with an added quality to thought. It bestows the capacity for lateral thinking, mental concentration and inspiration: the necessary non-liner solution or innovation simply bubbles up from the subconscious.

The bearers of good Mercury lines can really apply themselves mentally for long periods, give genesis to an idea, invent a new gadget, get the column written, find inspiration for the new advertising campaign. Such lines are found on journalists, writers, inventors, business people, comedians, and ideas people generally, though in such clear form such lines are rare.

More often than not it's found in its negative state: striated, islanded or trough-like. Physically, its connection is with the vagus nerve and its poor condition indicates an agitated nervousness interfering with the process of sleep, digestion, liver function and, particularly, enzyme production.

Where the line is fragmentary, digestive ailments are all too likely and the answer lies in relaxation and mental conditioning, e.g. meditation, not in antacid tablets.

When this line is deep and broken, it gives the sense of never feeling quite right, someone that suffers acutely from 'nerves' and often with a hyperawareness of the state of health. This may manifest as a macrobiotic diet fanatic or someone with a fascination with everything from fasting to homoeopathy. A striated form of this line is extremely common in the elderly.

Islands on the line exaggerate problems and, if the island should cross the Air line, some form of pulmonary complaint is likely: chest infection, pneumonia or asthma.

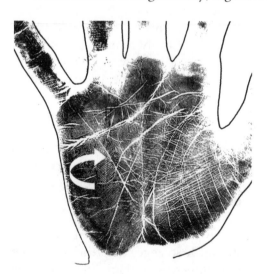

Illustration 141 A clear Mercury line – this is the hand of a journalist

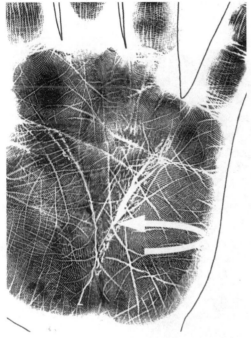

Illustration 142 A poor quality Mercury line. The hand of a man with a stomach ulcer and various 'nervous' complaints

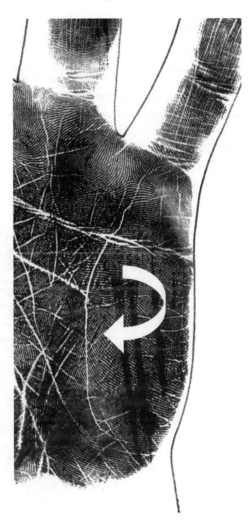

Illustration 143 A spirit line – this is the hand of medium Doris Stokes

It's always problematic when the Mercury line is very long and actually *crosses* the major Earth line – here, there's a direct neurological interference with the physical processes and life course. Illness is likely to occur (unless alleviated) at the chronological timing point where it strikes the Earth line. Check the Earth line's condition after the meeting point with the Mercury line.

A rare variation of this line is where it appears in a fine, long, curved form, then it's known as a 'spirit line'. This line plumbs all the feminine, subconscious awareness up to the realm of the communication digit. It's found more or less exclusively on mediums and extremely gentle, feminine people.

Mars line

This line is usually curved and is found on the inner Mars mount close to the thumb. Many people have a fragmented form of this line, but only when it's clear and longer than two centimetres or so does it take on the Mars-like qualities of red-blooded dynamism. It rules the liver area physically and its strong manifestation gives vigour and passion: it's prevalent amongst athletes, sports-people, aerobics instructors, martial artists and the like.

Its presence seems to give a high metabolism; they can pack food away and burn it off easily.

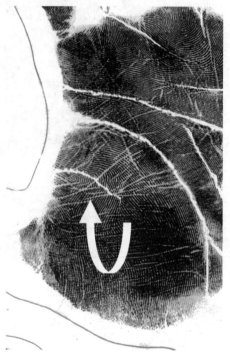

Illustration 144 A clear Mars line – the hand of a professional footballer

Even on a passive, sensitive hand there's an impression of intensity about the person. It's difficult not to be physically active with this line present.

Loyalty (family) line

This is a very common marking; it's not a true line but a broad crease or fold in the skin crossing the Venus mount from the base of the thumb to the Earth line. Its presence denotes an instinctive, tribal loyalty, which may be to anything from

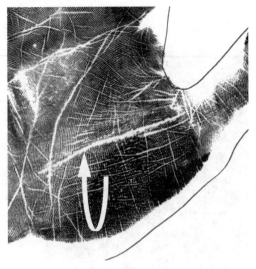

Illustration 145 A divorce marked by a 'splitting' loyalty line

the local rugby team, to partner, family or place. It usually indicates an interest in one's roots.

Where it's very strong, this faithfulness can go to considerable lengths (giving the children Manchester United team names, for instance). However, where it crosses and breaks the Earth line, this same fidelity will be found to be destructive.

This is a marker of a loyalty crisis and sense of betrayal. Typically it's a sign of divorce, a rending of the tie held so dear and consequent breakdown of stability, family and, possibly, health.

Intensity line

This is a fine, straight, horizontal line in the lunar quadrant. It's an energizer, it gives an extra buzz to the personality by creating a sort of stress in the subterranean emotional field. This line cuts off the depths of the sea of the unconscious, making it difficult for the person to really relax.

This line means that the inner responses need to be stimulated and stirred up; they have to *do* something to relax. It's found on people who need an emotional 'high', and it's surprisingly common on therapists, particularly those with an element of drama, such as art therapists or workshop facilitators. Meditation is very helpful to bearers of this line.

Thrill seekers, motorcyclists, people who love to party, body adorners, lovers of excitement and activity, all sport this marking. They will be unwilling and unable to truly wind down and are incapable of looking deep in themselves. They may well be drawn to dabble in drink, drugs, dressing up, role-playing and all the excitements of the night.

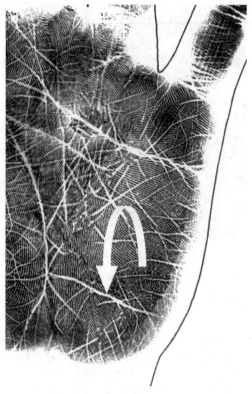

Illustration 146 An intensity line on a skydiver's hand

Allergy line (*via lascivia*)

This is a curved line, found in exactly the same place as the intensity line in the lunar quadrant. It indicates an over-responsive immune system and, generally, the presence of allergies. Where it's found, check the Earth line: if this is frayed, weak or islanded, there's an almost 100% chance of allergies.

It's a good idea to advise an allergy test for the major allergy response food groups, which are wheat, nuts, dairy products, seafood, red wine and chocolate. When it's strongly present, there can be cravings for the same foods to which they're allergic.

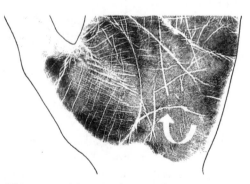

Illustration 147 Via lascivia line

Bars across the fingertips

If there are one or two of these, it's common enough and nothing to worry about.

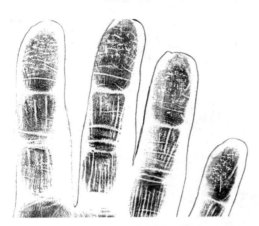

The endocrinal system is represented here and the fingertips are particularly marked on women's hands during the menopause. If the tips are much patterned with these marks, and it's not related to this issue, a high degree of stress will be present or ongoing endocrinal problems.

Bars on the mid-section finger phalanges are much marked when someone is inhibited or frustrated in their efforts to express themselves. Vertical lines indicate an extremely busy, active person.

Illustration 148 Finger phalangial bars; this is a woman undergoing the menopause

Many lines and grilles on the lowest finger phalanges (nearest the palm) indicate dietary problems or dissatisfaction with the body.

Samaritan lines (healing stigmata)

These are vertical fine lines, crossing the Water line under the little digit. They're associated with carers of all kinds – complementary therapists, nurses, healers, and simple 'good neighbours'. There needs to be four or more for a definite indication.

Illustration 149 Samaritan lines

Ring of Solomon

This cuts off the self-reflective mirror finger and allows insight into the nature of others. It bestows a natural inclination to analyse. It's found on perceptive personnel managers, advice givers, people who must handle others well. In its doubled form it's particularly insightful and is found on psychologists, astrologers and those who have a natural gift for understanding other people.

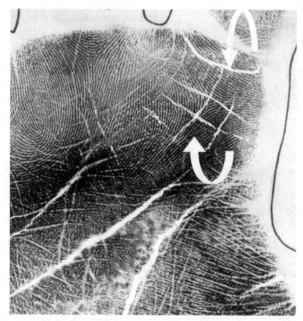

Illustration 150 Both a ring of Solomon and a teacher's square can be seen here

Teacher's square

This is a crude square made by lines under the index finger. Traditionally it's associated with teaching, but usually it simply reinforces the qualities of people management. It's common on teachers, but also on organisers and those with a sense of authority.

Aspiration lines

As previously mentioned in Chapter 7 (and see illustration 88) these are positive and can come and go quite quickly. They're little lines that rise up from the Earth line towards the index finger and represent a new job, new child, a better situation, positive attitudes and achievements.

One clear strong line represents a perennial determination to better oneself, often as a response to parental pressure.

Other markings

It's inevitable you'll find obscure lines, crosses, islands or other markings you don't recognise. Don't worry overmuch about these, as they can easily distract you from much more significant markings elsewhere on the major and minor lines. Always relate obscure markings to the area they're found on.

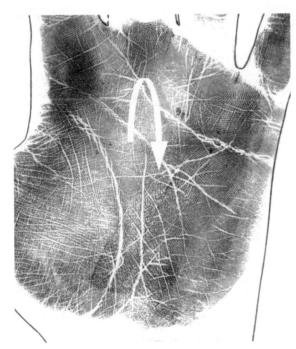

Stars are rare and indicate sudden exposure or publicity; bar lines crossing another line indicate obstacles; islands are an inability to comprehend and cope with a situation; squares are signs of rebuilding and protection; grilles are chaotic attitudes; crosses are positive decisions to be made in a conflicting set of choices; red dots are sudden flare ups, accidents and personal battles.

All such markings are highly transient, and may disappear within weeks.

Illustration 151 Chance line crossing Earth to the antenna digit

You can extract further information from the *location* of the marking.

For example, if a cross is found on the lunar quadrant, this must relate to a deep-held emotional situation that has reached a decisive crossroads.

A line crossing the palm from the Earth line to the antenna finger area, will be some sort of stressful connection between the home, family and health (Earth line) and commerce, study, or sex (antenna digit). So the line here informs you about, for example, the demands of a university course or a business project or sexual interest interfering with stability, home and health.

Always bear in mind where a marking is found, the type of marking, and the general hand features, before responding to them. But again, don't get in a state about them – even the most experienced readers ignore such nondescript signs.

EXERCISE

Congratulations! You've covered all the ground and are now almost ready to launch yourself on an unsuspecting world!

Go through the minor lines again carefully, over and over until you're sure of their meanings.

Go back through your print collection and work through a complete interpretation of the hands of four people you know. The closer you are to a person, the harder they are to read because you have so many subjective assumptions. Your own palm will be most difficult of all. Write out the readings, give them to your 'victims' and put their feedback in your journal.

10

Putting it all Together

The real magic of hand reading begins here, when you test out your skills and assimilate all the various points to make a complete picture of the individual. We'll enhance your abilities further by refining your intuitive perceptions, which everyone possesses to some degree.

Now perhaps you'd like to try a simple test to reinforce your understanding. Take a deep breath, and examine the handprint in illustration 152.

You've seen this before; it's the hand we looked at the end of Chapter 3. It's the active palm of a middle-aged woman. Study this print carefully and refer to the text where necessary in order to answer the following questions – the points to check are given in each case. (Answers can be found at the back of the book.)

How does this person see herself? Check the balance of mirror and peacock digits, and the print on the mirror digit.

What can you say about her emotional life? Check skin texture, any markings in the lunar quadrant and the strength, length and nature of the Water line, plus any mirage and affection lines.

Is she highly motivated? What sort of work might she do? Check the thumb qualities. Also look at the qualities of the Fire line and the length of and print on the wall digit. Check also for palmer loops of industry or leisure.

How far you've come! Now you possess the key to unlock the secrets of any hand. There are, of course, a huge number of further qualities to be extracted from this hand, including, crucially, a comparison of the active and passive hands to see the full range of the personality. For now though, you need simply to build up your experience – let's go!

Psychological traits

Below, you'll find some personality traits and the relevant hand indications to look for. This should really get you thinking. Bear in mind that without these indications the qualities may well be latently present. One indication is enough to give an

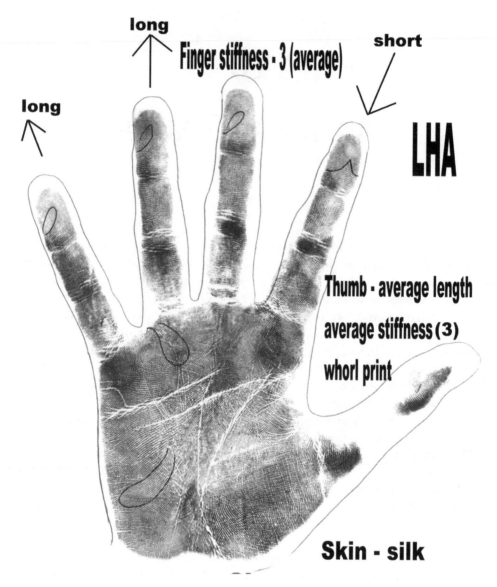

long

Finger stiffness - 3 (average)

long

short

LHA

Thumb - average length

average stiffness (3)

whorl print

Skin - silk

Illustration 152 Test hand print two

aspect of the trait mentioned, but it will be especially marked where you have more than one.

Remember that indications made by lines are subject to change.

Acquisitive/materialistic

Look for: Earth hands; index or all fingers bent towards the middle finger; a Fire line that starts from the Earth line; a short, straight Air line; a 'bridge' line above the end of the Air line; all fingers curling inwards towards the palm; a Water line rising to the middle finger.

Adaptable/flexible

Look for: highly flexible fingers and a flexible jointed thumb; a narrow palm; composite prints on thumb or index, or all digits sporting loop prints; an uprooted or weak Earth line; the absence of a Fire line; the absence of simian or semi-simian formations; and no lines completely crossing the palm.

Ambitious

Look for: a Fire hand; a long, strong thumb and/or a long index finger; little aspiration lines rising from the Earth line; a large gap between the Earth and Air lines; simian lines.

Artistic/creative

Note that everyone is artistic in some degree. Look for: a Water hand; a long ring finger; a mirage line; silk skin; a loop of sensitivity; a loop of inspiration; a whorl in the lunar quadrant; a clear, curved Water line; an Apollo line; a bulging lunar mount; a well developed Venus mount; a curved Air line; whorls on the ring digits. (Note that by artistic, I refer to the traditional meaning of art – 'to craft or fashion; to aspire to the divine or the beautiful'. This doesn't apply to conceptual art: Turner Prize candidates for instance usually sport extremely cerebral qualities, with poor quality Water lines and signs of emotional inhibition.)

Ascetic

Look for: Air hands; knotty fingers; short Water line; small basal finger phalanges.

Assertiveness/authority/confidence

Look for: a strong thumb or a long index finger; bold red lines; a well defined, straight Air line with a large gap between it and the Earth line; naturally wide spread fingers; a strong Fire line.

Compassionate/caring/a therapist

Look for: a flexible jointed thumb; healing stigmata; a long, straight Water line; a Water palm; silk skin; a radial loop on either hand's index finger.

Confusion

Look for: a long, striated mirage line; a 'full' hand with multiple lines; an islanded or poor qualilty Air line; composite prints anywhere on the hand; the lack of a Fire line.

Control freak/obsessive

Look for: a long index finger; very stiff fingers; a long stiff thumb; whorl prints on both index and thumb; a simian line.

Criminal tendencies

Criminals display the qualities of low self-esteem, intensity, rebelliousness and a significant lack of empathy. The following indicates the possibility of aberrant behaviour when two of more of these qualities are present. Look for: markedly short index fingers; very stiff fingers overall; coarse skin; a short, poor quality, straight Water line; an overlong ring digit; a short middle digit; partial or complete simian lines; Air line connection to Mars mount.

Diplomatic/conciliatory

Look for: a long Water line; Water hand; a mirage line; silk skin; composite prints anywhere on the hand.

Eloquence/language skills

Look for: a long, straight or slightly bent little finger; a long, clear Air line; an Air hand; paper skin; a writer's fork.

Energetic/restless/dynamic

Look for: an intensity line in the lunar quadrant; grainy skin; a Fire hand; a Mars line or a loop on this mount; deep, straight, red major lines; lots of whorls; a strong, stiff thumb and stiff fingers; a Sydney line or simian line.

Fun loving/pleasure seeker

Look for: a loop of leisure; hyperflexive thumbs and fingers; large basal phalanges; a short Earth finger.

Intuitive

Like creativity this is a universal trait but it will be much closer to the surface with the presence of the following: A Water hand; a radial loop on the index digit; silk skin; a loop of sensitivity; a spirit line, an Apollo line; an Air line curving deep into the lunar quadrant.

Jealousy/inadequacy

Look for: a simian line; rigid fingers; a short index finger; dropping lines at the end of the Water line toward the Earth line.

Nonconformism

Note that everyone likes to think of themselves as nonconformist. The following, though, will guarantee inherent difference. Look for: a short middle finger or a whorl on this digit; lots of whorls generally; a strong Fire line or one curving from the lunar quadrant; a clear mirage line; a very long Air line; any unusual prints in the Water quadrant.

A touch of magic

Now that you've learned the practicalities of palm reading, lets add a little sparkle to the process and introduce the intuitive facility. This will illuminate our perceptions and allow us to open to a more universal viewpoint.

Intuition is a perfectly normal, latent human ability available to some degree in anyone.

When you start to give 'live' readings (with the person you're reading for actually present) you'll find yourself becoming more finely attuned as you forget yourself and concentrate on them. You'll pick up subtle glimpses and impressions that are on the edge of your awareness. When honed and refined, this subliminal level of perception can really bring a reading to life, adding resonance and colour.

This facility must be carefully developed and controlled. However, it's all too easy to get carried away: 'I'm getting the colour pink'; 'I'm picking up something happening in your sacral chakra'; 'I feel there's a lot of karmic stuff going on with this relationship'; 'You will meet someone and definitely be married to them by next June'.

These are all genuine quotes by various so-called palmists, overheard at Mind, Body and Spirit fairs. Please don't let yourself give waffly, woolly-minded readings like this, unless you're reading goat's entrails!

To read from only your intuitive response is haphazard, often untrue, frequently irrelevant and generally, plain silly.

Your aim should be to work with both right brain hemisphere (intuitive, non-verbal), and left brain hemisphere (verbal, structured) simultaneously.

Wolfgang Smith's discovery of the benzene ring, Leonardo da Vinci's flying machines and Isaac Newton's revelation of the nature of gravity, are all well documented examples of intuitive 'flashes', allied with structured intelligence.

Insight, even genius, comes from keeping the mind open like a child's to fascination and wonder, while simultaneously being alert to the rational facilities. In this way one may come to know 'those sudden breaks in the clouds that sends the soul aloft on angels wings to new heights, new visions' (Isaac Newton, *The Principia*).

You've already learned to give an astounding reading through structured analysis; now we'll deepen the process a little.

Meditation

In order to keep the mind receptive, we need to develop the quality of 'inner listening'. This is the quality of keeping the mind 'soft' and awake to subtle impressions.

In the increasingly stressful world we inhabit, however, we can only do this when we've learned to still the mind from the blizzard of thoughts and mundane mental 'noise' that blinds us most of the time. We accomplish this through meditation.

Meditation has become has become a little rarefied and precious in recent years; the preserve of the initiate and the monastery.

You don't need to become a Buddhist or do yoga to benefit from meditation. It's straightforward enough and the benefits are endless.

Meditation is simply the practice of allowing the mind to gently hold it's focus on a sound, object or passive activity and to keep it there, ignoring the thoughts that arise and the distractions that are always present.

Illustration 153 Inner listening

The practice

The first thing you need to do is establish a regular time and place for your practice. Don't worry about statues and shrines, joss sticks and candles; these are props and can be helpful, but aren't essential. Don't worry if you can't get complete peace and quiet; learn to focus in distracting circumstances.

Try to get comfortable, without necessarily being in a classic lotus or kneeling posture. It's fine to be lying down (if you don't find yourself getting sleepy), otherwise sitting on a stool, a pile of cushions or in a chair with a straight back is best.

Put on some soft background music; you might like to try something by Mozart (Mozart has been proven to stimulate alpha mental states, the most receptive to intuition), but any relaxing music is suitable.

Now select the focus of your meditation. A good, basic practice is to close the eyes and become absorbed with all the subtle sensations of the movement of the breath in the nostrils – the warmth of exhalation, the cooling inhalation. But by all means try contemplating, with half-closed eyes, a flower or crystal, a basin of water or any object you choose to place in front of you.

Whatever the centre of your attention, reach out and mentally 'grasp' softly with your mind and hold the focus. No matter how many times you get lost, keep coming back to the focus of attention. This is the spadework of meditation. Every time you do so you become mentally clearer, dispersing the clouds of distraction.

Keep the mind 'soft' and relaxed; reach out with the gentlest, lightest touch. Don't get annoyed with yourself if you find you've been thinking about what you're having for lunch for the past five minutes. Tenderly come back to focus, softly stay on course, lose the sense of beginnings and endings.

Try to have a sense of being all in this moment, completely involved in this process; the greatest treasure is here and now, not in the yearning for any experience other than this one.

It's vitally important to understand that meditation is *active*, and dynamic: the activity of constantly keeping the mind 'soft' and bringing it back to the object of attention. It's not about being lost in distraction, nor daydreaming, nor getting into a 'nice inner space', however enjoyable. It's to reach out mentally and hold your attention still – it's as simple, and as difficult, as that.

One of the greatest drawbacks in meditation is the ambition to 'get somewhere'; particularly the ambition to become enlightened, or to open up the kundalini, or indeed to become psychic. These desires are actually destructive – the very act of trying to *attain* anything is a part of the distraction. Don't yearn for or chase these experiences, or feel disappointed if you don't have them.

After around fifteen minutes or so, let go of the meditation object, but keep the music playing and sit peacefully for ten minutes, enjoying your newly-found calm.

This period after meditation is when you go into 'inner listening'. This is a process of just letting the mind drift and watching what impressions arise. This is the state in which the intuitive facility is at its most receptive.

Don't mentally 'snatch' at ideas; just watch what floats into consciousness. Write these impressions in your journal.

When you've found your favourite section of music, make sure you always have this same 'signature piece' playing when in meditation and in sitting quietly afterwards.

After a week or so the 'inner listening' process can be extended to other activities; try to retain this quiet attention state at will, while you're actually *doing* something: walking, talking on the phone, washing up. Play your 'signature' music to trigger the inner listening state; relax and let your mind become soft and open, let yourself be inspired.

After a month or so of practice, integrate this process into a 'live' hand reading. Have your special music playing either quietly in the background or through a Walkman.

The mind will quickly associate the music with the receptive state and will remain open and attuned.

Ensure you stay relaxed and receptive while working through the levels of analysis, paying particular attention to your breathing – keep it as slow and deep as possible and the gaze should be soft.

Let your mind dance over the various layers as you read through them. Start with the shape and skin and work steadily onward; be confident, be gentle; never hurry.

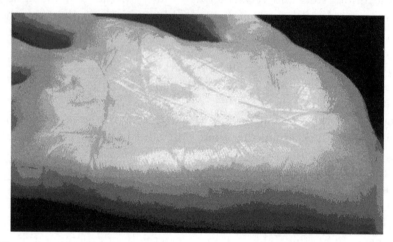

Illustration 154 Opaque hand image

Now use your inner 'listening' to give specific examples of the character qualities and experiences of your client without allowing yourself to feel under pressure to be right or to impress.

The intuitive capacity should be used in a reading only within the rational framework of what you've uncovered through observation, and always, but always, prefixed with a 'perhaps', 'this could be', 'for example' or other proviso.

For instance, you note the very short index finger and while commenting on this you get the impression of a child being bullied in a playground. Of course, you already know the very short index is indicative of sense of inadequacy so: 'There's a problematic self esteem issue here, it might have been that you were bullied at school?', would be a good and illustrative example to use within the knowledge 'frame'. If the intuitive example is wrong, it doesn't matter: the statement is crucially true in itself.

You can give similar illustrations of any palmer feature, with as much detail as you can furnish. On the client's Apollo line, for instance, you might state: 'you love to withdraw to a kind of inner stillness, it may be that you like to sit on a bench in the garden and watch the fish move in the pond?'

Always start your example with a proviso like 'perhaps', 'maybe' or 'it's possible that' to suggest rather than claim a fact.

This form of example giving is particularly resonant and important when it comes to the past and future. You may note the break half way along both the Water and Earth lines, plus the falling affection line and you get the impression of a suitcase, or an airplane, for example. To the young, married client you could say: 'There are very big changes marked further on. This could mean very different life circumstances in the future, unless you take steps to stabilise your situation. For instance: the future could involve a move abroad'.

Again, the breaks in both lines and the falling affection line would indicate a very strong likelihood of a divorce and life change, and the 'for example' means you're not committing yourself, nor frightening the client with definite prediction.

Your intuition can, as always, provide the *illustration of the particular events signalled by the palmer indication.*

Perhaps you've found a very disturbed beginning of the Water and Air lines, and an unrooted Earth line on the passive hand. While describing the qualities of these features you may, for instance, find the image or impression of a soldier floats to the back of your mind. Here you might then say: 'Your early life seems to have been a little unstable and ungrounded, did you perhaps have a parent in the armed forces so the family had to move house a lot?' Again, your inner listening *illustrates and exemplifies your indications.*

Using intuition within logical frameworks is an extremely rich and powerful form of reading. Most importantly, you're not limiting and corrupting a person with fixed messages of the 'you're going to marry in June' variety, nor confusing the vulnerable with 'lots of karmic stuff with this relationship' nonsense. Your examples will free you from the frightening determinism and mumbo-jumbo of less able readers.

Sudden inspirations will come to you ever more readily as you get more relaxed and gain experience. Let's say during a reading while looking at the long ring finger you get the impression of someone playing tennis. If there's a developed Venus mount (physical drive) or a large Mars mount or Mars line marking (competitive), a mention of tennis as this person's particular skills would probably be spot on. However, if this impression doesn't seem to fit with the hand you're reading, or the aspect you're describing, *don't mention it*. You don't want to load your client with irrelevant detail you don't have a frame for.

Even when you don't feel particularly inspired, it's good to get into the habit of giving examples to colour your readings. With practice and by staying relaxed and 'listening', your readings will become more accurate, powerful, and resonant.

Keep your signature music playing and keep your mind open, so that inspiration will come to you. If you feel drawn to a particular line or marking that seems to 'speak' to you, allow yourself to respond intuitively, always maintaining a keen eye on the rational 'frame'.

Eventually you'll be able to 'tune in' easily, and read without the music playing. A good reading requires a sort of balancing act, with both left and right brains feeding and filtering impressions, neither side being allowed to dominate. Pure logic can be aloof and mechanical, pure feeling can be gushy and over-sentimental. Using the convergence of open receptivity and rational insight will produce the magic of the true master.

A palm reading should be moment of clear-sightedness and heightened awareness for both reader and client. In this way a reading becomes not a confrontation with a fixed destiny, but a moment of revelation, opportunity and change.

EXERCISE

Practise the meditation and inner listening for a couple of weeks. Go over all the previous chapters to reinforce them. When you feel sufficiently ready, take your courage in both hands and plunge into your first 'live' reading. Make sure you're in your own, calm environment with the signature music playing. Don't get nervous, explain you're still learning, stay calm, stay open. Keep this book handy as you may need to refer to it.

11

Different Dimensions

Now that you're in the position to read hands you're going to be very popular!

Palmistry has its rules and guidelines, just like in art or engineering. Such a devastatingly powerful tool must be wielded carefully and the guidelines provided here will help you in the actual practice of palmistry. You'll also learn how to angle the reading differently according to what you're looking for in the hand.

Before you let the world beat a path to your door though, let's set out some basic reading principles.

- Readings are always about helping people, not entertaining them. Try to liken a reading to a counselling session. Put difficult points subtly. Rather than pronounce negatives like: 'you have terrible levels of self esteem!' to the person with a very short index finger, you can ask 'do you feel you didn't have much positive reinforcement as a child?'
- There will always be sceptics to challenge you and others who will be impressed beyond measure. Never be arrogant, pompous or above anyone; like writers, hand readers must immerse themselves in life, not be aloof from it.
- We all have problem areas and flaws, but we can be liberated from them by understanding. Get the person you're reading for to contribute. Balance difficulties with inspiration to develop their natural attributes and talents. The rule is: don't take anything away from a person without giving something back.
- It's a good idea to record readings; people often swear you said something you didn't!
- Giving a reading is an incredibly personal experience, and your client may feel that no one knows or understands them as well as you. Be aware of your responsibilities, never take advantage, never, ever, use palmistry to form an intimate relationship with a client.
- If you read at a professional level, make sure you offer a money back guarantee. Very few dare make such an offer in this kind of business, and it will be your customer's assurance that you're no fraud. I was terrified when I first offered this guarantee some fifteen years ago; in fact I've returned one person's fee in

all that time (not because the reading was inaccurate, but because the client didn't like what she heard!). Your high standards and integrity will mean you need have no fear.

- Be humble, keep learning. Put your feminist, socialist, anarchist or conservative opinions to one side while reading. The hand is a universal form of truth, it can't pertain to an ideological viewpoint. The truth is bigger than you are!
- Inaccurate self-perception is one of the cornerstones of suffering.
- You aren't expected to see and know everything!

If time is limited, you can do ten-minute 'quickie' readings, without taking a print, just look at the skin texture and the qualities of the index fingers and thumbs, particularly the dermatoglyphics on these digits. This gives you crucial information on the individual's receptivity, drive and sense of self.

Performing readings at 'psychic fairs' is a wonderful way to gain experience. Here again, there isn't time to take a print, just look at the shape, skin, fingers and dermatoglyphics and the strongest line. Or the same basics and the most outstanding feature – that short water line for example, or maybe that simian line.

In a longer, private reading, take a print and try to cover everything. Move slowly through the frames of reference in the same order as presented in this book. Remember that the presence of silk skin, or a composite print pattern on the thumb, or very bent Air line may be the key to unlock the person from their lifelong confusion.

If you find yourself reading only, for instance, nurses and carers, and never read businessmen, you may need broader experience. Try to read for types that are different from yourself.

Remember that human nature is full of contradictions. This is what makes us such incredible, magical, multi-faceted individuals. That person with a long index finger (strong self esteem, self aware), a very poor Fire line (lacking clear personal goals and values), a short 'tied' Air line (limited vision, orthodox) and a lot of whorl prints (independent, original) may be thrashing around helplessly, unable to make sense of their experience. You are their navigator, following the map of their soul, helping them to find their own way.

A good reading technique is to read to the nature of the person you're looking at, as reflected in their Air line and skin quality. Its no good suggesting massive life changes, for instance, if someone has the 'tied' Air line of a cautious, timid personality. Nor talking in a poetic, symbolic manner to someone with coarse skin and a short, straight Air line. Better to be practical and direct.

Remember that lines and dermatoglyphics draw on the energy of the mounts or quadrants they're marked upon. If an area is of exaggerated size its qualities will be magnified by a print or line upon it. For instance, if the inner mars mount is enlarged, and there's a loop print on it or a mars line, the forces of that area will be very strongly activated. Similarly, a strong earth line will manifest the energy and power of a large Venus mount.

Contrary patterns

A peculiarity of human behaviour that makes hand readings so valuable in a fluid society is *contrary* patterns. Contrary patterns are those behavioural traits which compensate for a weakness, making a person appear to be something they're not.

For instance; someone with a very weak Earth line (ungrounded, insecure) may extend all their energy in acquiring great wealth, so that they compensate for their innate unrootedness with materialistic security. Don't be surprised, therefore, to find that people of high status – government ministers, heads of department – will often show hand indications, not of practicality and self discipline, but of the fear, aggression or insecurity which drives them.

This contrary pattern can take a more subtle form in, for example, the way that obese people often display disproportionately small index fingers. They become very large physically, where they actually feel innately small and insignificant.

There are endless further examples: the man with a very short middle finger (unorthodox, unstable) may become an army officer in order to acquire boundaries and structure. Without such discipline he may go off the rails with his innate non-conformism. The person with a Water line that runs right across their palm may spend a lot of time alone, because they can't stop responding to the demands of others. It's important to be alert to these 'contrary' examples, where people are compensating for innate vulnerabilities.

People, as you will see, are full of such ironies and complexities.

I was amazed when I read the hands of a group of yoga students to find how stressed they were; the answer is, of course, that this is what drove them to the practice.

If you trust what you see in the hand and not the exterior appearance, you will always be true.

Bear in mind that the values that commonly constitute the popular ideal of success aren't necessarily those that make a person happy and balanced. Indeed, success in the modern world often demands that we relinquish stability and re-invent ourselves on demand, transforming ourselves into what's required. Economic prosperity and high status may not constitute being true to what you are.

The most fulfilled, happy and balanced people aren't film stars or Nobel Prize winners, but are generally found living quietly in chalet bungalows, cultivating prize-winning roses.

Don't ever make assumptions as a reader. Don't assume, for instance, the Earth-handed person in front of you with very few lines is some sort of Neanderthal throwback, and that every bearer of a long fingered, multi-lined hand is a natural genius; they aren't. The uneducated, Earth-palmed Greek fisherman can be a font of natural wisdom and the Air- handed doctor of philosophy woefully confused.

Hand reading remains the most mind blowing, liberating, magical and confidence building practice known; it's the process of people really getting to know themselves.

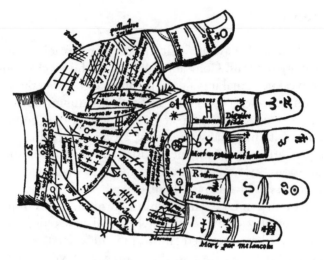

Illustration 155 Classic palmistry print

It's said that the very best readings tell the person exactly what at some level they already know. As they are the source of all that you discern, this must indeed be true.

Wield your wisdom gently, leavened with tact, subtlety and compassion.

As a budding master palmist, you need to get as much practice as possible to build up your experience. We'll use some more advanced techniques now, examining the hand from various perspectives. We can look at the palm differently depending on what qualities you're looking for.

Emotional and sexual qualities

Assistance with love and relationship situations is probably what most people want from a palm reader.

The passive hand is particularly important in relationships, because we tend to reveal this inner, more vulnerable aspect of ourselves to those we're intimate with.

Looking at an individual from an emotive angle always starts with the skin quality because this provides the basic level of receptivity. A silk-skinned person would respond to candlelight and innuendo, where the route to a coarse-skinned person's heart would be rather more rough and ready!

The Water line – its quality, length, curvature and ending – is obviously vitally important; this tells you much about a person's emotional patterns and needs. A straight, red Water line emotes very differently (and more urgently) than someone with an islanded, broken line. Generally, two people with similar Water lines are compatible emotively. However, if the palms are markedly different (a Fire hand with coarse skin and a Water hand with silk skin for instance) the two people will inhabit two different realms and will never be compatible.

Look for any affection lines reaching into the palm. The mirage line, if present, also affects relationships and must be considered. Examine the sense of self as presented in the index fingers and the drive represented by the thumbs. You must look at these, because in any relationship the issue of dominance will arise. A person with a long stiff thumb and/or a long index finger will often dominate a partner, unless they have equally strong digits.

The prints on the index digits reveal much – a whorl on the index digit will mean the person will find it difficult to see themselves as part of a partnership, particularly if both passive and active index fingers bear whorls. Conversely, someone with a radial loop on the index finger will need commitment and lots of reassurance from a partner.

Look at the little finger and see if it's low-set and look for the presence of a passion line. Passion is also indicated by an intensity line in the lunar quadrant and a Mars loop or Mars line. The Earth line and Venus mount are worth consideration in terms of the sense of security and general 'oomph'. Note any marking in the lunar quadrant, like a composite or whorl, and any unusual qualities of the Air line.

A mysterious process seems to operate in respect of the emotions, in that we seem to radiate subliminal signals, attracting the emotional experiences we generate within ourselves. If we are insecure and unromantic, we attract an insecure and unromantic person. Consequently, any improvement in the inner condition attracts a better and more fulfilling love life. Checking out all these points will enable you to do a great emotive and sexual analysis and also to see if two people are compatible.

Vocational analysis

It's not advisable or necessary to specify a *particular* career for any individual, as we're all capable of a wide range of skills. But you certainly can ascertain a *field* of work ideal for a person from their hand. Again, the first place to start is the skin, coarse-skinned folk want stimulating, active work while silk-skinned people want to work with their feelings. Any definition of hand shape allied to this will narrow things down considerably. Someone with an Earth hand and coarse skin would go bonkers chained to an office chair; similarly, a Water-handed, silk-skinned person would have a nervous breakdown in the army.

Of particular importance are the markings between the digits – the loop of leisure and the loop of industry. One with the former would need to enjoy their work and ultimately wouldn't sacrifice social and pleasure concerns for the career, while the latter marker will incline them to take work seriously.

The print on the middle digit is important – it defines the attitude to work. The overall pattern of the prints generally point to the method of working: if there are lots of loops, these are great team workers; lots of whorls love to be unsupervised or self-employed and to specialise in a niche area; carers and therapists tend to have radial loops on the index digits, and arch prints people like to work in practical, useful, emotionally non-demonstrative roles or with manual and craft skills.

The lines of Fire and Air are crucial in vocational guidance. A long Air line would need to contribute ideas and communicate in work, someone (depending on shape and skin) like a teacher or a garden designer, where a short straight line would want to be in a more applied business realm.

If the Fire line itself is missing, this would signal that a person is unable to define their career path as yet and they should go for a job that gives structure. Where the Fire line is present, remember that a line from the lunar quadrant is inclined towards the artistic, personal and social, where one from the Earth line is more traditional, orientated to following the rules, hierarchy or canon. Breaks in this line often indicate career change.

Long Fire fingers need risk and creativity and the ability to show off somewhat, where a long index finger needs control over a small, co- operative and generally more conservative realm.

When giving advice on career, remember that we can't all be artists, healers and therapists; many prefer the stability and security of a regular salary. Do take practical and domestic issues into account.

Spiritual readings

The spiritual aspect of a reading can only be defined by understanding what you actually mean by spirituality. To some this may mean regular church attendance, to others it may mean meditation practice. Some consider spirituality to mean one is intuitive; others may follow the dictates of the Koran to the letter. Clearly, none of these definitions is entirely satisfactory.

Perhaps a good definition of spirituality might be taken from Kahlil Gibran's *The Prophet*, where he describes spirituality as 'to realise the best, purest and most universal essence of the human'.

We can, and will, realise this 'universal essence' when we can access all parts of our consciousness without compulsion, fear, repression or ignorance.

The only unprejudiced and useful spiritual definition from a hand reading point of view is to recognise that all movements towards self-improvement and self-knowledge are a kind of spiritual process and that true spirituality must pertain to some kind of balance.

To attain balance means to work on one's *weakest* aspects; this is the key to a spiritual reading. The hand lends a privileged overview, where we can really guide a person usefully.

If you're looking for a holistic balance, you can easily see that the young Jehovah's Witness with the tied Air and Earth lines may be intolerant and narrow-minded, or that the person with an ungrounded, half-present Earth line and escapist mirage line off to yet another meditation retreat, needs to actually get a job and support herself. This is hardly the news they would want to hear, but nonetheless this is the only way for them to grow.

Any line may be overlong or overcharged and too strong and this is as much a problem as one that is weak or broken.

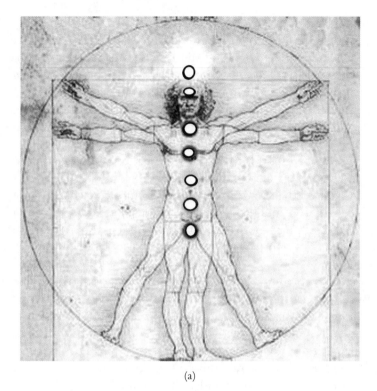

(a)

Illustration 156 (a) The chakras

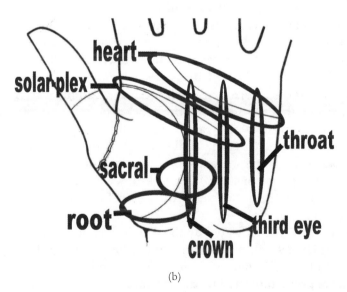

(b)

Illustration 156 (b) The chakras – crown, third eye, throat, heart, solar plexus, sacral, root

When a minor line, like the Apollo line, is over strong and the Earth line weak, you may get, for example, an overweight psychic with poor health, whose reserves of energy are expended in 'channelling spirit'. The most beneficial spiritual activity would be, in this case, to diet and exercise rather that channel dead uncle Alistair, however much they protest that their own path is the correct one.

One can see in the palm a symbolic representation of the chakras. This is a straightforward but effective method of reading the condition of these spiritual/energetic centres which are placed along the axis of the spine.

The **root chakra** corresponds to the bottom section of the Earth line. It relates to grounding, base, Earth, solidity, fundamentals, basic life needs, body survival, fixidity. If the base of the Earth line is missing, the root chakra is weak. They'll be ungrounded, spaced out and materially dependent. If the line is deeply marked and red in colour here, the chakra will be too strong, making them fixed, immobile and stubborn with too great an association with survival and the basest instincts.

The **sacral chakra** corresponds to the central portion of the Earth line. It relates to sensual pleasure, our attitude to the body in terms of pleasure, diet, food and sex; digestion, and in a woman, the womb. If this section is islanded, missing or broken up they may confuse sex and food and may have weight problems; there's a poor attitude to one's own body and physical beauty. Inhibitions abound in the expression of natural femininity or masculinity, sense of attractiveness and simple creativity. If very deep and red, or with branches here, it indicates an obsession with exercise and the body beautiful.

The **solar-plex chakra** is expressed in the Air line. If clear and strong, it's reflective of the strong expression of will through the solar-plex and means that personal vision, opinions, character and purpose are strong. If the line is weak and bent, the solar-plex lacks drive, character, vision and application, and the person finds it hard to direct and assert themselves effectively.

The **heart chakra** is represented by the Water line and shows the capacity of feelings of universal love, objectivity, self-sacrifice and empathy. If too long and strong, it shows one that's supremely caring, but who can't say no and is too self-sacrificing. If the line is short or weak, it signals this chakra is functioning poorly, with an over-rational, unfeeling materiality and lack of awareness.

The **throat chakra** is represented by the Mercury line or spirit line. If poor in quality it represents poor concentration, lack of wisdom, insight and originality. If found clear and strong, the strength of this chakra gives wisdom, insight and universal understanding.

The **third eye chakra** is indicated by the Apollo line. It is clear presence indicates creative vision, second sight, inner illumination, loss of ego and a retreat from the material. A lack of this line indicates this chakra is undeveloped.

The **crown chakra** is illustrated by the presence of the complete Fire line, running from base to the top of the hand with all the previously mentioned chakras (represented by the other lines) being in good condition. This would represent the rising of the kundalini from base to crown and an almost god-like sense of completion. This line in its complete form, with all the other chakra areas in good, clear condition, is seen perhaps once or twice in a lifetime and usually on exceptional individuals. My own two examples are on a Buddhist monk and a lifelong yoga devotee and guru.

Note that this is a fairly crude reading method – any complete analysis would have already picked up these points. The easiest chakra diagnosis is simply to look at the one or two chakra areas that stand out as particularly strong or weak.

EXERCISE

Now you need to build up your experience of 'live' reading as much as possible. Try to read everyone and anyone you possibly can. Try to do at least a reading a day. Have a go at looking at the hand from the perspectives in this chapter. Don't rush! Practise, practise, practise and then practise some more!

12

Health in the Hands

Palmistry from a health perspective is a relatively new phenomenon, driven to a large extent by scientific papers published in recent years. While this is an important and fascinating aspect of analysis, this is an optional aspect of study and great care must be taken with the knowledge gleaned.

The hand gives advance warning of the onset of most disease processes.

It's easy to terrify people with any statement in the area of heath. Because you're working with the mysterious dominion of the palm, people may take any statement you give as a covert prediction of imminent illness. For this reason, be extremely careful, always remembering that unless you're medically qualified you should *never actually diagnose any condition*. Merely advising a healthy lifestyle (low fat diet, high in unprocessed and natural whole foods, low alcohol intake, not smoking, regular exercise) will go some way to alleviate most conditions.

Often a problem registers on the hand at a very early stage, before it can be ascertained by conventional health screening.

At a genetic level, many scientific papers have been published linking specific dermatoglyphic patterns to a predisposition to develop a particular disease. However, as far as a reading is concerned, informing someone of their propensity to a disease is of little use unless they can actually *do* something about it.

Some indications are listed here, with linked condition and preventative advice. Bear in mind if you have these dermatoglyphic markers you have only a *statistically greater likelihood of developing the disease* and most people with these indicators *won't necessarily develop the condition*.

Nine or more fingertip loops

Alzheimer's and senile dementia. Prevention: high intake of omega fatty acids, mental exercise, e.g. crosswords puzzles and study. Immune system disorders. Prevention: Echinacea and pycnogenol pine bark extract, both potent immune boosters.

Three or more fingertip whorls

Eye weaknesses: myopia, development of cataracts. Prevention: Bates Method eye strengthening exercises, avoid direct sunlight and eyestrain.

Whorl prints in the lunar quadrant

Schizophrenia. Prevention: Avoid use of marijuana, avoid becoming isolated from other people.

Three or more simple arches on the fingertips

Intestinal obstruction, constipation and intestinal disorders. Prevention: high fibre diet, avoid junk food, regular exercise.

Four or more whorls on the fingertips

Congenital heart disease. The most important indicator of congenital heart disease, however, is a displaced axial triradius (where it's placed higher up the palm than normal, even if this is a second triradius, or it's displaced by a loop or other marking).

A displaced axial triradius is also the single most important indictor that a person may produce a Down's Syndrome child, bearing in mind that Down's Syndrome itself is sign of congenital heart defects. Prevention: low stress lifestyle, don't smoke, low cholesterol diet.

Skin ridge decay and the nature of disease

The great hand reading pioneer, Noel Jaquin, discovered that where the skin ridges appeared to be breaking up, this signalled bacterial infection and the onset of the disease process. You may already have noticed this smudged, eroded look on areas of some of the prints you've seen.

Now the illuminated magnifying glass really proves itself. Through the glass, healthy skin looks like a series of raised lines of unbroken ridges.

In certain areas these ridges may be eroded and look, when magnified, like a series of dots. There may be fine 'veiling' (which is a plethora of very fine lines), so that skin ridges may have the appearance of being erased away.

Different areas correspond with various organs and physical systems. Broken up skin ridges signifies an infection, or less than optimum conditions in the organs which correspond with the part of the hand the decayed ridges are found on.

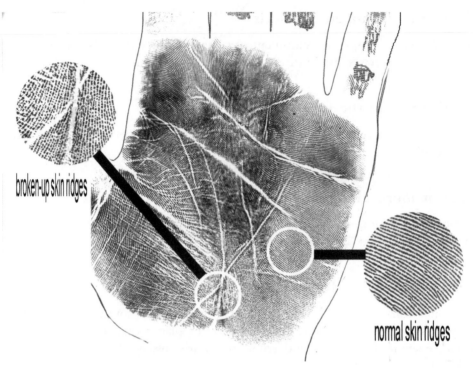

Illustration 157 Normal skin and broken-up skin ridges

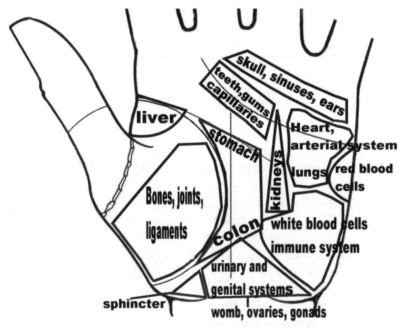

Illustration 158 Areas of the palm and the corresponding organs

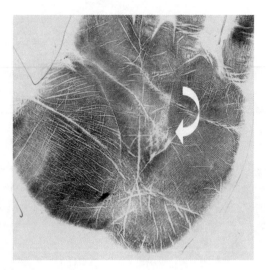

Illustration 159 This man had a kidney transplant three weeks previously; note skin ridge break up in the corresponding area

The nails

The nails are particularly indicative of a person's general physical condition and must be examined with care. The individual nails grow at slightly different rates – faster on the active hand than on the passive, and faster on the thumbs, slowing in growth rate as you move around the digits to the little finger.

Healthy nails are pale, rose-pink in colour, unmarked by ridges, white spots or grooves with a natural sheen to their surface. They also have a natural curvature and clear moons.

Any marking on the nails is only significant if the sign appears on *more than one nail*, otherwise it could merely indicate an injury to the nail bed on that particular digit.

White spots on the nails are common (called leukonychia punctata). They signal that the person is mineral deficient, run down and probably suffering sleeplessness. They're prevalent on nursing mothers, junior doctors, shift workers, teenagers living on anxiety and late nights, and on those recovering from illness.

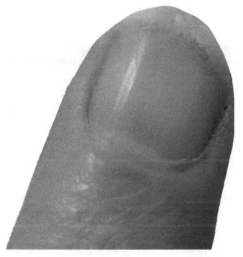

Illustration 160 A healthy nail

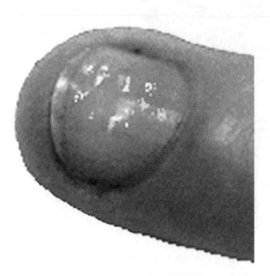

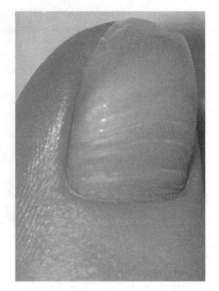

Illustration 161 White spots on the nails   *Illustration 162 Beau's lines*

One or more ridges (Beau's lines) running horizontally across the nails, like a wrinkle in the surface, mark a period where nail growth was interrupted in previous weeks. This is usually through temporary illness, but it could be from some other shock to the system, e.g. an accident, surgical operation or emotional trauma.

A series of much finer, longitudinal lines are common and a sign of general anxiety, over-activity of the nervous system, adrenal stress and an early warning of rheumatic and arthritic disorders.

Tiny, pin-prick like indentations on the nails are symptomatic of long-standing skin diseases, like dermatitis or psoriasis. Streaks of brown discoloration in the nail, usually near the top edge, point to uric acid build-up and some sort of renal (kidney) problem. Check for skin ridge break up under the ring finger.

Deep red nails indicate the possibility of high blood pressure, where very pale, bluish or purple coloured nails indicate the possibility of low blood pressure, circulatory or cardiac problems.

The nails can droop, rather like the leaves of a failing plant. If you hold the fingertips six inches in front of your face (as if about to poke yourself in the eyes) and look square on at the nails, their profile should be curved and the nail's rim shouldn't droop or be flattened out. If the nails are flat in profile and, particularly, if the edges droop, there is general long-term fatigue and lack of vitality; not serious or necessarily illness-related, but the body needs rest and rejuvenation.

The lack of moons on the nails is very common (they're always present on the thumbs), but it shows that aerobic capacity and circulation aren't optimal.

Digital clubbing is the where the tips of the fingers swell like drumsticks. This is often accompanied by Hippocratic nails – swollen, dome-like nails, lifted from the nail bed and drooping at the ends, often with a bluish colour. Where more than three digits have this sign, it's a signal of a very severe and advanced illness, probably a condition of the cardio-vascular system, and they should be advised to see a doctor immediately.

Now let's look at some other disease indicators. These signs signal the likelihood of a problem being *actually present,* rather than a predisposition. Most diseases have their roots in some

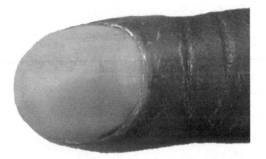

Illustration 163 Digital clubbing

way in stress conditions, so first check for signs of this in the palm. Advising people to adapt a slower pace of life can prevent many illnesses getting a grip when only the warning stress signs are evident. Indicators of stress are: a 'full hand' with multifarious lineation; multiple stress lines crossing the Earth line; an island or large break in the Air line; a striated or overdeveloped Mercury line; a

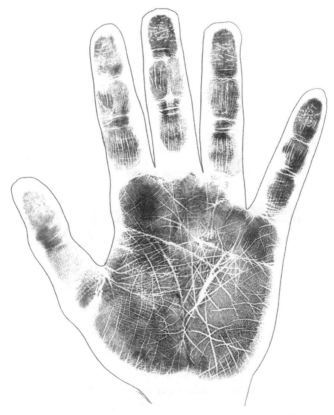

Illustration 164 A palm displaying all the signs of stress

short middle finger; plentiful lines in the lunar quadrant; bars across the top finger phalanges; simian lines; lines linking the Air and Water lines; very stiff fingers.

Health conditions and indications

Anaemia or poor circulation

Very cold hands and pale skin; white nails and pale lines with no colour, even when the palm is stretched out.

Allergies

Presence of an allergy line; a poor quality, striated Earth line.

Bladder/gynaecological problems

Lots of tiny lines or skin ridge break up in the base of the lunar quadrant.

Cardiovascular/circulatory problems/heart failure/lung insufficiency

Hands very cold and nails bluish in colour; red dots in the Water line under the ring digit. A hard knot of skin under the ring digit and on the Water line, which looks as if the line's erased, is often a sign of arterial blockage or restriction to the heart. Hippocratic nails; digital clubbing.

Debility

Island at base of the Earth line.

Dementia

Island at end of the Air line.

Depleted vitality

Weak lines; flabby hands; tasselled ending to the Earth line.

Diabetes

Muscle wastage in the inner Mars mount (the small muscle visible at the back the Mars mount when the thumb is closed against the palm); also a line from the Mars mount (near the thumb) joining the Water line.

Digestion problems

Very deep, striated or doubled Mercury line; an islanded, weak, striated or broken Earth line; skin ridge break up around the Venus mount and down the front of the Earth line.

Endocrinal disorders

Indicated by cross lines on the top phalanges on all the digits (very common during the menopause). Individually, the little fingertip has been linked to the thyroid; the ring fingertip with the thymus; and the top phalange of the thumb to the pituitary gland.

High blood pressure

Nails and lines a deep red colour and hands very hot and pink.

Intoxication of bacterial origin

Skin ridge break up around the Earth line.

Irritable bowel syndrome

Veiling lines and skin ridge break close to the Earth line; weak striated Earth line.

Jaundice

Yellow skin and nails; island in the Mars line.

Kidney disease

Veiling and skin ridge break up below the Water line under the ring finger.

Multiple sclerosis

Hand tremors and an island in the Air line

Pulmonary disorders

An island on the Mercury line where it crosses the Air line.

Thyroid problems

If the hands are hot, moist, smooth and silky, there is an overactive thyroid. If it's underactive, the skin is cold, rough, dry and doughy.

Illustration 165 Medieval gypsy palm reading print

Now you're equipped to read anyone's hand. You're a soul perceiver, a mind-mapper, a lamplighter of inner darkness. Keep practising, never stop learning. As you begin the business of hand reading, the best tools to carry are an open mind and a sense of humour. To understand another better is a step towards loving acceptance, and of this there can never be enough. Remember Shakespeare's dictum that 'we humans are but giddy things' and a dash of humour will leaven this rather serious business of analysis tremendously. No one, after all, will escape alive from the human condition and we are all but children, blindly fumbling towards the light.

Appendix

Biblical references

Exodus 13:9 'And it shall be to you as a sign on your hand'.
Proverbs 3:16 'Long life is in her right hand and in her left riches and honour'.
Job 37:7 'He seals up the hands of every man that all men might know his work'.

Answers

Chapter 2 – Celebrity hands quiz

A. Princess Diana – Water; B. Puff Daddy – Fire; C. Milosovic – Earth; D. Bill Gates – Air.

Chapter 3 – Print test

This is an Air hand. This person would be likely to be physically tall and gangly. At the most basic level, this person's nature would be predisposed to independence, rationality, communication and refinement and specialisation, and the realm of ideas. He or she would question everything and is likely to be someone that works things out for themselves. Assuming the person had the opportunity of a good education and that other features do not contradict this quality, he or she might make a good teacher, communicator, media person, or planner; someone who 'writes the script of life' in some way. He or she would need space and freedom and would possess a latent non-conformist streak.

In reference to the silk skin texture he or she would be highly receptive, sensitive and intuitive. They'd respond to 'vibes' and atmospheres, tuning in to the subtle inference of their surroundings. They would naturally avoid conflict, and prefer gentle, harmonious situations.

At first sight, this isn't a particularly outdoorsy type, and this person isn't likely to make a particularly good heating engineer because they are not pre-disposed to manual work and the limitations of the material, repetitive and mundane worlds. A sensitive, cerebral environment would be better – like counselling work. This person would be great at advising others, or using ideas in a spiritual/caring/imaginative/creative/receptive manner.

He or she'd certainly be sensitive, and perhaps prone to stress.

Chapter 10 – Print test

This is just a brief summary of the main points. Of course, we're committing the ultimate chirological crime here, in that we're only reading one palm and in effect only reading half the person. Nonetheless, this will show you how far you've travelled in your insight and power.

We've ascertained this is a middle-aged woman, that this is an Air hand and that the skin is silk in quality. The shape and skin have already been discussed in the answers to the previous test. Now let's look at the other qualities presented. The thumb is average in most respects, except that there's a whorl print on it. This will make her a self-starter, someone independent who will do things her own way. She's got a self-motivated attitude and will brush opposition aside. There's a love of innovation and originality, she'll trust her own experience over the expertise of others. Independence is a strong trait, given that this is an Air palm which will exaggerate this tendency.

The short index finger informs us there are self-esteem issues present. She doubts herself at a deep level, though she probably covers this with a confident exterior and avoids introspection. She's a middle child, or one that had to perform for attention. Deep down, she may well need encouragement, though this would only be evident in one-to-one situations. The tented arch print on the index finger signals a dynamic intensity and edgy nervousness to the personality. She wants excitement and extreme experiences. This marking is found on those who teach, entertain or motivate others so this may be part of what she does. She needs to learn how to relax.

The ring finger is of exaggerated length, giving the capacity for showing off, creative expression and social kudos.

The little finger is of similarly extra length and this makes her a lover of words and language, someone with a large vocabulary and with good business skills, wit, and abilities with language. Physically, the skin quality is silk, so there's a need to be particularly careful about her environment in terms of foodstuffs, disharmony and stress. She's very sensitive.

Career-wise, the Fire line indicates she wouldn't have made her own career choice and will work in a field lain down by her parents or convention. This isn't someone who has left school with any kind of a career plan of her own. The Fire line connecting to Earth means career choice was limited to what was on the table. This would have frustrated her natural drive for freedom (Air hand) and her need to do things her own way (whorl on thumb). The loop of leisure on the palm would have further complicated matters, as she'd need work she enjoyed doing, or would want time off for hobbies and holidays. Fun and fulfilment would ultimately win out over pure career issues.

Work then would need to be conventional (Fire joined to Earth) be of a specialist, idea orientated nature (Air hand) that didn't challenge her sensitivity to her environment (silk skin) with excitement, and the ability to be on the stage of life (long ring digit and tented arch print on index) with scope for independence of expression.

Emotionally, she's extremely inhibited and emotionally unaware (look at the very short, straight water line). She's pragmatic and black and white psychologically (straight Air line), not someone who'll beat about the bush. She suffers tremendous, almost psychic sensitivity to her environment (loop of sensitivity, silk skin) yet emotionally in her relationships with others and herself, she's blunt, direct, and un-emotive, she has a limited range of feelings and is hard to know.

Her intensity (tented arch print) and her limited ability emotionally would make her a lively talkative person with tremendous ability to tune in to others yet unable to really connect with them in any personal or intimate way. It's likely she'd have negative expectations in relationships and may suffer divorce (you may be able to make out the falling affection line).

OK. There are loads more points to be extracted here, but here's a brief biography of our 'victim'.

She's a celebrity health expert who gives people dietary and lifestyle advice in makeover-type programmes. She's known for her blunt and forthright style and perceptive ability to tune into her clients. She's trained in the family profession of nutrition – both her parents were health experts. She's written books and gives speeches to large groups of people. She has a strong sense of drama – needing both excitement and lots of time to relax. She has loads of hobbies and doesn't like to work too hard between the demands of her diary. Her independence and originality are evident in that she combines alternative and conventional health advice, she's something of a maverick to the traditional approach to nutrition as she herself was taught. Relationships are unfortunately 'a disaster area' in her own words – she's been divorced twice and finds it hard to get really close to a man. She's childless and though she has loads of friends there are few who are really close. Her relationship with her mother is interesting. She's a middle child and feels she's still trying to come up to her mother's high standards and never felt good enough or loved unconditionally.

Bibliography

Brandon-Jones, D., *Your Palm, Barometer of Health*, Rider, 1985.

Cummins and Midlo, 'Dermatoglyphic analysis as diagnostic tool', *Medicine*, **46**, 35.

Cummins and Midlo, *Fingerprints, Palms and Soles*, New York, Dover Publications, 1943.

David, T. J., 'The palmer axial triradius, a new method of location', *Human Heredity*, **21**, 624.

Denton, B., 'Principal component analysis of the elongation of the metacarpal and phalangeal bones', *American Journal of Physiological Anthropology*, September 1977.

Digby Role 1V, 13th Century Ms, Bodleian Library, Oxford.

Greenough, Black and Wallace, 'Experience and brain development', *Child Development*, **58**, 539–559, 1987.

Hale, A. R., Phillips, J. H. and Burch, G. E., 'Features of palmer dermatoglyphics in congenital heart disease', *Journal of the American Medical Association*, **1176**, 41.

'How to build a human' BBC2 TV programme, Sunday 27 January 2001.

Hummel, F., 'Ipsilateral cortical activation of increasing complexity representation', *Clinical Neurophysiology*, April 2003.

Hutchinson, B. *Your Life in Your Hands*, Sphere, 1967.

Jaquin, N., *The Hand Speaks*, London, 1942.

Jones, C., *The Interpretation of Dermatoglyphic Patterns*, Swan Paradise, 1992.

Manning, J., 'Long ring digit, pointer to autism?', *New Scientist*, March 2001.

Manning, J., 'Depression index', *American Journal of Evolution and Behaviour*.

Manning, J., 'Sex role identity related to ratio of 2nd and 4th digit in women', *Biological Psychology*, February 2003.

Manning J., 'The ratio of 2nd to 4th digit length and performance in skiing', *Journal of Sports Medicine and Physical Fitness*, December 2002.

Manning J., '2nd to 4th digit ration and offspring sex ratio', *Journal of Theoretical Biology*, July 2002.

Manning, J., 'The ratio of 2nd to 4th digit length – a proxy for testosterone and susceptibility to AIDS?', *Medical Hypotheses*, December 2001.

Napier, J., *Hands*, Allen and Unwin, 1980.

Penrose, *Recent Advances in Human Genetics*, Churchill, 1965.

Putkin, B., 'Diagnosis of clubbed fingers', *The Lancet*, September 1996.

Raham, Q., 'Sexual orientation and the 2nd to 4th finger length ratio: evidence for organising effects of sex hormones or developmental instability?', *Psychoneuro-endocrinology*, April 2003.

Scheimann, E., *Medical Palmistry*, Aquarian, 1989.

Shuster, C., 'Digital arches in digestive disorder', *American Journal of Gastroenterology*, August 1997.

Wolffe, C., *The Hand in Psychological Diagnosis*, London, Methuen.

Web-sites

The web is awash with palmistry sites, unfortunately many are a mixture of psychobabble and superstition. A couple of good sites to get you started are:

www.handresearch.com
www.handanalysis.co.uk

My own web site at www.johnnyfincham.com will provide you with an up to date list.

Index

Active hand 3
Adaptability, signs of on the palm 62, 109
Affection line 114
Air element 22
Air line 85
Alchemy, its use of the elements v, 16
Allergies, signs of on the palm 123, 152
Ambitious, signs of on the palm 79, 91, 94, 129
Anaemia, signs of on the palm 152
Antennae digit (little finger) 50
Apollo line 117
Archetypes 23
Arch print 62
Artistic, signs of on the palm 65, 68, 129
Ascetic, signs of on the palm 129
Aspiration line 124
Assertiveness, signs of on the palm 219
Astrology
    knowledge of iv
    use of the elements 16
Asymmetrical hands 4
Axial triradius 68

Bar lines 75, 125
Beau's lines 150
Biblical references to palmistry 155
Bill Gates' palm 25
Bladder problems, signs of on the palm 152
Brain – relationship to palm 2, 34

Brain development and the fingers 44
    proportion of nerves devoted to the hands 1
Brandon-Jones, David 158
Breaks in lines 75

Cardiovascular problems, signs of on the palm 152
Cerebral cortex 44
Chakras, their representation on the palm 143
Chance lines 125
Changing lines on the palm 2
Character 104
Cheirology vii
Chi 73
Chirology vi
Circulatory problems, signs of on the palm 152
Coarse skin 31
Communication skills, signs of on the palm 7, 50
Compassionate, signs of on the palm 100, 129
Composite print 58, 60, 63, 64
Confusion, signs of on the palm 129
Cosmic ocean 60
Criminal tendencies, signs of on the palm 130

Debility, signs of on the palm 152
Dementia, signs of on the palm 76, 146

Depleted vitality, signs of on the palm 152
Dermatoglyphics – on the index finger 61
  as indications of disease 146
  little finger 66
  middle 64
  ring 65
  thumb 63
Diabetes, signs of on the palm 152
Digby Role vii
Digestion problems, signs of on the palm 152
Digital clubbing 150
Digital triradii 69
Digits – length 40
  leanings 42
  stiffness 42
Diplomatic, signs of on the palm 130
Disease, signs of on the palm 146
Divorce, signs on the palm 74, 77, 100, 101,
    113, 121
DNA 2
Down's syndrome, signs of on the palm 52,
    68, 95
Dowser's loop 70
Dyslexia, signs of on the palm 90

Earth element 16
Earth line 77
Einstein's hand 88
Elements 16
Eloquence, signs of on the palm 50, 130
Endocrinal disorders, signs of on the palm
    152
Energetic, signs of on the palm 130
Equipment for print taking 9
Evolution – and finger development 34
  thumb development 34
Exercises 13, 26, 33, 39, 56, 72, 95, 109, 125,
    136, 145
Extroverted, signs of on the palm 37

Fate line 104
Fingers – bar lines 75
  knots 54
  leanings 42
  length 40
  phalanges 53

print patterns 57
  stiffness 42
  tips 54
Fingertips, shape of 54
Fire element 20
Fire line 103
Fixed palmer features 14
Flexible fingers 43
Fun loving, signs of on the palm 130

Genetic patterns 3, 14, 57, 146
Grainy skin 30
Gynaecological problems, signs of on the
    palm 152

Hand
  shape 14
  size 5
Head line 85
Healing stigmata 123
Health indications 146
Heart failure, signs of on the Palm 152
Heart line 98
Hepatica line 119
High blood pressure, signs of on the palm
    150
Hindu palmistry 39, 57
Hippocratic nails 150
Hyperflexive
  hands 43
  thumbs 37

Idealistic, signs of on the palm 43
Illness, signs of on the palm 146
Index finger 44
Insecurity, signs of on the palm 79, 92, 98,
    101
Insensitive, signs of on the palm 31, 99
Intensity line 121
Intoxication of bacterial origin, signs on the
    palm 147
Introverted, signs of on the palm 42, 113,
    117
Intuition, development of 131
Irritable bowel syndrome, signs of on the
    palm 153

Index

Isaac Newton 131
Island on a line, meaning of 75, 125

Jaundice, signs of on the palm 153
Jealousy, signs of on the palm 101
Journal keeping 13
Jung, Karl, theory of the subconscious 16
Jupiter mount 9
    finger 44

Karmic patterns 57, 162
Kidney disease, signs of on the palm 165
Kirlian photography v

Leukonychia punctata on the nails 150
Lifeline 77
Lines – major lines 73
    markings on the lines 75, 125
    minor lines 111
    subsidiary lines 125
Little finger 50
Long fingers 15
    long antenna 50
    long mirror 44
    long peacock's feather 49
    long wall 47
Loop of industry 67
Loop of inspiration 70
Loop of leadership 67
Loop of leisure 67
Loop of mystery 69
Loop of nature 69
Loop of rhythm 70
Loop of sensitivity 67
Loop prints 58
Loyalty line 120
Lunar mount 7
    quadrant 8
Lung insufficiency, signs of on the palm
    153

Major lines 73
Markings on the lines 75
Mars mounts 8, 9
    line 120
Materialistic, signs of on the palm 128

Meditation 132
Menopause, signs of on the palm 152
Mercury quadrant 7
    line 118
Metacarpals 15
Middle finger 47
Milosovic's palm 25
Minor lines 111
Mirage line 112
Mirror finger 44
Moons on the nails 150
Mounts 7
Multiple sclerosis, signs of on the palm 153

Nails as health indicators 149
Neptune 111
Non-conformism, signs of on the palm 131

Obsessive, signs of on the palm 130

P. Diddy's palm 25
Palm
    broad 14
    narrow 14
    shape 15
    size 5
Palmer – lines 73
    dermatoglyphics 57
    skin 27
    markings 57
Palmistry principles 137
Paper skin 27
Passion line 115
Passive hand 3
Peacock's feather digit (ring digit) 49
Percussion area 7
Phalanges 53
Planetary and non-planetary names ix
Pointed fingertips 54
Poor circulation, signs of on the palm 152
Princess Di's palm vii, 25
Print taking 9
Psychological qualities, signs of on the palm
    127
Pulmonary disorders, signs of on the palm
    153

Quadrants 5
Quiet listening 133

Radial loop print 61
Readings
  giving a reading 137
  reading practice 136
Relationships 98, 140
Retreat line 82
Ring finger 49
Ring of Saturn 112
Ring of Solomon 134
Rings on the fingers 52

Samaritan line 123
Saturn line 112
Schizophrenia, signs of on the palm 147
Self-esteem, signs of on the palm 44
Self-reflection, as seen in the mirror digit 44
Sensitivity, signs of on the palm 29, 114
Sexton, Anne, quote 29
Sexuality 101, 140
Short fingers – short mirror 45
  antennae 51
  peacock's feather 44
  wall 47
Silk skin 29
Simian line 94
Simple arch print patterns 61
Skin
  coarse 31
  grainy 30
  nerve endings 28
  paper 30
  ridge density 28
  silk 29
  texture 27
Spatulate
  fingers 55
  thumb 38
Spirit line 120
Spiritual
  development 142
  analysis 142
Squared-off fingertips 55
Stiff fingers 43

Stress indicators on the palm 151
Stress line 82
Striation
  of Earth line 80
  of major lines 73
Support lines 82
Sydney line 90
Symbolic representation of the digits 43
  of the major lines 73

Teacher's square 124
Technique, developing 127
Tented arch prints 60
Thumb
  angle 37
  development 34
  length 34
  print pattern 63
  stiffness 35
  tip 38
Thyroid problems, signs of on the palm 153
Timing on the Earth line 84
Travel lines 81
Triradii position 68
  normal 68
  missing 69
  normal 68
  raised 68

Ulner loops 60
Undifferentiated hands 23

Vagus nerve 119
Venus mount 8
Via lascivia line 123
Vocational analysis 141

Wall finger (middle finger) 47
Water element 18
Water line 98
Web-sites 159
White spots on the nails 150
Whorl of isolation 70
Whorl print 61

Zones of the palm 5